LOVE DANCES

H&A Publishing Company

All rights reserved. No part of this book may be reproduced or transmitted in any form or by any means, electronic or mechanical, including photocopying, recording, or by any information storage and retrieval system, without the written permission of the publisher.

Copyright© 1992

H&A Publishing Company
4820 Alpine Place, Suite B202
Las Vegas, Nevada 89107

Library of Congress Catalogue Card Number:
　　95-95231

Heffner, Van V., 1945-
　　Love Dances
　　ISBN 0-9649610-0-8
　　Inspirational

Printed in the United States of America

H&A Publishing Company: October 1995

If unavailable in local bookstores, additional copies of this book may be purchased by writing the publisher at the above address or by calling 702.878.8832 or faxing 702.878.5009

Dedication

This book is dedicated to my wife, Joan, and our daughters, Amanda, Emilia and Katherine, who assisted me in setting free the spirit of the little boy inside of me. This book is also dedicated to the spirits of the children in all of my brothers and sisters, in the true essence of God, in every land.

My life's purpose is to share Love and be caring in creating peace and harmony in every person and throughout the world. God is with us along every path, as one chooses, Love Dances.

Contents

Author's Note	ix
Dancing With Spirituality	1
Dancing With Children	5
Dancing With Adolescents	9
Dancing With Adults	12
Dancing With Parents	16
Dancing With Grandparents	20
Dancing With Your Family	24
Dancing With People From Other Lands	28
Dancing With Music	32
Dancing With Art	36
Dancing With Friends	40
Dancing With Feelings	44

Dancing With Dating	48
Dancing With Marriage	52
Dancing With Learning	56
Dancing With Money	60
Dancing With Fun	64
Dancing With Dogs, Cats & Roses	68
Dancing With Birds, Bears, Trees, Mountains & Streams	72
Dancing With Courage & Risk	76
Dancing With Care	80
Dancing With Judgments & Nerds	84
Dancing With Joy & Magnificence	88
Dancing With Perceptions	93
Dancing With Forgiveness	97
Dancing With Trust	103
Dancing With Winning	107

Dancing With Excellence	111
Dancing With Success	116
Dancing With Sexuality	120
Dancing With Sexual Intimacy	126
Dancing With Birth	132
Dancing With Service	136
Dancing With Your Body	140
Dancing With Food	144
Dancing With Alcohol	149
Dancing With Drugs & Smoke	155
Dancing With Death	161
Dancing With Peace & Harmony	167
Dancing With Vision	172

The illustrations in this book are reproduced from original drawings by the author.

Author's Note

On a Sunday morning during January 1992, I was driving home with my eldest daughter to Las Vegas from Salt Lake City. Amanda was sleeping in the back seat after our incredible experiences on a rope's course with my sister, Sue Heffner, brother-in-law Frank Carman and friends.

While driving past the shadows of Mount Nebo in radiant sunlight of a midwinter Utah sun, a vision of inner peace and harmony warmed my body from head to toe. The inspiration swirled around me as a white light, soft and gentle, yet it was the greatest power I have ever experienced.

My heart warmed with unconditional Love for my wife Joan, our daughters, family, friends and every person, animal and plant. The spiritual freedom of Love soared to an incredible energy level, which was first expansive then focusing into a guiding message from God to create harmony and peace for all.

The vision was clear, write a book without judgment, to serve everyone in creating inner peace and harmony. An entire book about life and all parts of it, flashed through my mind. The warmth continued with softness,

LOVE DANCES

lightness but always clear and strong as the title, "Love Dances" floated in the car in the radiant white light of day.

Amanda awakened experiencing the same warmth, Love and spiritual freedom of the moment. We shared stories of the preceding days' events and returned to small talk, plans and happenings as the energy shifted. I didn't give any more thought to "Love Dances," other than to share the title and experience with my family.

On Monday, in the early morning hours, I awakened to an incredible warm feeling in my fingers and a soft, gentle feeling in my heart, that was both serene and powerful. I went to my computer, thinking about my experience that day before and began to write. Chapter titles flew through me as if channeled from a higher being, deftly and in an incredible exactness that was truly amazing. Each day, shortly after midnight a chapter or parts of a chapter would come to me, inspired as only God might guide one. Inspirational messages about every part of life were so strong, yet without judgment, limitation to languages, religions or cultures. Forty chapters later, the inspirational book is complete, with only minor editing as it was shared with me.

Author's Note

I give you, <u>Love Dances,</u> as it was Lovingly shared with me. May it serve you as much as it has me, my family and friends. Enjoy it and share its inspiration to create Love, peace and understanding.

On a given day, a chapter or chapters will softly and gently touch your heart, let it serve you with inspirational guidance and read that chapter or chapters. The power within will guide you in making choices, which will serve you in any part of your life.

Kay Carman, my beautiful mother-in-law, was truly inspired through the vision of "Dancing With Courage & Risk" at that special time in her life as she went on to heaven. This or other chapters will bring clarity and light to you for that special moment or circumstance in your life.

Let your heart experience the Love, inner beauty and spiritual peace of <u>Love Dances.</u>

Dancing With Spirituality

As one looks into their inner spirit it is realized that a wonderful life experience has been chosen. God creates incredible opportunities for all to enjoy the dance of freedom and special lessons to attain that freedom.

The choice of life comes to each new born child, choosing its parents and the experiences that it will have as that child dances through a unique and soaring life. Opportunities of spiritual growth occur every day throughout this chosen life of family and friends in its chosen world.

The dances that are learned are ever changing as is the spirit of the child. This spirit never dies as it continues its quest of freedom, service and creation of new birth. This spirit is Love and a part of God, and grows as the God within one grows.

Nurturing God through Love, opens doors for new

LOVE DANCES

dances. These are dances of new adulthood, special relationships, marriage and children.

Intimacy is chosen as the spirit reaches its highest energy created for that special moment when all stands still, while renewing a spirit through birth and the new child's focus to learn new steps. These are dance steps for new experiences, new opportunities to enjoy abundance through service, employment, money to fuel a worldly lifestyle, and a commitment to share with Loved ones.

Our own world is created, no matter how small or how vast. It extends with no limits into the universe where Love can soar free with the spirit's choice.

There is no end or no beginning to this universe, but it contains all, including our family, our own home, our church of choice, our country with its own chosen politics, and our heaven. God is with us along every path, as one chooses, Love Dances.

Your spirit is the soft inner voice energizing our bodies, our minds, our feelings from our hearts. The heart of life is the soft dance of Love that creates more Love, more life, and a world where all can live in peace and harmony.

Dancing With Spirituality

Our world, as we choose to dance in it, is made up of dogs, cats and roses, as we dance with our pets, in our gardens. Every moment we create our world, enhancing the given place, with the strength of God.

Birds can soar, nest and live in harmony with mother nature. Bears dance on a log to catch a salmon sustaining its body and allowing the salmon to be free to energize a new life in a new way.

As you choose to plant a tree or harvest one, you choose life for one and the opportunity for others to grow in pure radiant sun light, standing strong and proud. Caution is shared as you harvest too many you will steal the life thriving balance of the trees' forest, placing stress and pain, possibly death to the soft balance of that special forest where animals and birds dance with each other, sharing it with all who choose to dance among the leaves.

Our mountains embrace us with protection and life; replenishing the earth, through a kiss with each cloud; sharing cleansing thunder, lightning and rain; recycling all to create new life, growth and abundance. Each mountain contains its own mix of minerals and strength to share a dance of a diamond, gold or mother earth, shining a million facets of light and life, regally through its gold

Love Dances

or the soil to sustain the grass and wheat to feed all, from our cows to our ducks and to each of our families in our chosen homes.

The blankets of life from the mountains velvet each valley for the dance of life to continue. Caution, again is shared, as each mountain and valley shares its abundance, each spirit chooses the gift of Love in replenishing each mountain, valley and stream to be sustained and to be enjoyed.

The soft balance is there for all to share. Commit your inner spirit to protect the environment to assure the cleansing of the earth, erasing destruction of our world and enjoying the diamonds, carefully shared, and golden grain to continue life for eternity.

Dancing With Children

A child is born totally free. A spiritual child, with the true essence of God, chooses its parents and family, with other people in a chosen land, where the new spirit can grow and learn to soar.

Unconditional Love and trust abound in this child without judgment, but with total courage to share all with one's chosen family and friends. This spiritual courage energizes the child to seek others of its kind without restriction or limit.

From the first minute of the first breath of this child, Love is shared and Love is sought, to create an inner energy so strong, yet so soft, that this Love fuels the life path that has been chosen. As Love is shared and nurtured, the child creates this new chosen life of peace and harmony.

The path of this chosen life offers unlimited challenge and opportunity for the child. A life of traditions, a life of

LOVE DANCES

growth, a life of lessons, a life of teachings, a special life is unique to the chosen, dancing among the flowers to the sounds of the birds singing freedom for all to enjoy.

As the child crawls, walks and runs along life's path, shared by God, opinions and comments are made by the elders, teaching the child the dance of expectation. Sometimes this dance restricts the openness and freedom of the inner spirit of the child. Aging follows birth, as does the creation of the social expectations of the child with one's chosen people.

The child's dance for universal freedom changes as new, and often different steps are learned. The free movement may become limited or restricted as the expected traditions cast the veil of judgment, discipline and pain on the free child.

The soft inner voice of the child knows the dance of its chosen life. It becomes fearful of rejection, fearful of failing to fulfill the vision of the taught future, not the future to totally Love and to share the joy of freedoms.

Dreams of soaring free are dimmed by the elders. The child grows and ages, until walls of limits shroud the blessed child each year, as the child grows toward adolescence. The smiles dancing across each child's face become expected, changing from free and honest to those of expectations.

As the child dances with its youth, it dances with all of the people in the chosen land. It dances with teachers, church leaders, friends, and at holiday celebrations including that special birthday of life, spiritually chosen many years ago.

The soft inner voice of the child knows that this chosen path offers an abundance of growth. The dance of the people, with whom the child lives, creates an ever-growing energy to interact with the ever-changing child, preparing this child to flow into adolescence, prepared to fulfill the dreams of new life and new partners.

The child dances along with the wonderful memories of a well-nurtured and safe life. Traditions have been shared, traditions have been learned and the inner spirit remains free to dance into the teenage years with a knowledge of expectations.

The child casts a different Love to trust in a learned way, with new lessons that have been taught. This special child holds the unconditional Love inside, protected, yet totally real, growing with God as it chooses new dances that have been chosen with the ways of the people in the

Love Dances

chosen land.

Joy and fun still abound within the child, but in a new way, dancing to the newly learned music of life from the chosen parents. The newly learned steps exude confidence for the child to dance with friends and life in the sunlight and with the stars, twinkling that special radiance shared among this child, its parents, family, friends and all its chosen people.

Dancing With Adolescents

The dance of the spirit, as it transcends from childhood to adolescence, is as individual as it can be steeped in tradition. It is that special time when physical sexuality begins and the ability to recreate oneself becomes possible as the spirit chooses.

Adolescence for the newly found teenager becomes a time to dance with dreams of who we are and who we are not. It serves the spirit well in creating a different being and yet a being that can be totally alike.

The energy of spiritual individuality grows, exploding into one's own freedom, while totally leaving all the traditions of the elders, the learned ways of childhood and casting new limitless energy to dance among the chosen people with its own grace and uniqueness.

The soft gentle spirit, in the presence of God, retreats to the safety of childhood for one fleeting minute holding that unconditional Love that has always been there. A

Love Dances

new minute dawns and the spirit exerts its new power, projecting the vision of the future adulthood far beyond its earthly years, abruptly changing all around it. Safety and cares dance away with the breezes of a new found being, powerful, yet gentle, as the sun embraces new light and warmth each day for all the chosen people in the chosen land.

As the years pass from childhood to adulthood, adolescence serves as one dances from one time to another space. The physical appearance changes along with the learned dance of the people.

One sex leaves its own kind and creates flirtatious dances in its own unique way, soaring before all whom it might attract. The sexuality mounts, energizing the teenager to fulfill an inner desire to share in that special moment of complete intimacy when all stands still and life is again created, and a new spirit joins this special world from the universe.

The teachings of the people, as they are in the chosen land from one's chosen parents and family to the churches of choice, and from the politicians establishing the laws of the land, encourage the dance of caution to the adolescent. The spirit, finding its own sexuality as a teenager, has the choice to fulfill a greater life through a commitment to maintain each spirit's respect, allowing all other dimensions to be shared.

The partners each teenager attracts, in their new found dances, are searching to share all, through an expression of their deepest inner feelings, values of comfort, intellect of success and dreams for a future of unlimited Love. Love that does not always appear as it is, but as it can be.

The adolescent dances with all of its dreams, its newly found sexuality and carefully founded values, some of choice, some out of rebellion from the choices of others in the chosen land. The dance soars to a new height, as the beauty and grace of the teenager is set free to soar like the eagle above and beyond the shimmering waters of the lakes and streams, beyond the free spirits of the people in every land and with their own soft inner Love that is always there to guide it carefully and safely into adulthood.

Dancing With Adults

  *T*he ever-changing vision of the spirit, with the essence of God, moves freely from adolescence to the wonderful realm of becoming an adult. Physically mature, emotionally growing, intellectually creating and spiritually soaring, the dance of adulthood begins, as the pleasures and pains of adolescence fade into one's past.

  The adult shines to a new dance of living forever, being able to accomplish all and opportunities to choose to share with every other spirit so finely connected with others in the chosen lands of its universe. The dance has the beat of youth and the vibrations of parents that will soon be fulfilled as the connection of coupling serves if the adult so chooses.

  Meaningful and totally, fulfilling solo dances are wonderful for those to choose as they focus their life in service of one's family or to one's chosen people in their chosen community. The solo dancers may choose to share with a potential mate or a dancer like themselves, serving others in the same way they serve each other. Some solo spirits, though still softly and securely connected to all others, commit their lives to their church of choice, a mission for their chosen country, or a family member or friend, relying on their strengths to fulfill each other's lives.

Other adult spirits, again softly connected with all other spirits, unite with their chosen partners dancing at their wedding, celebrating the commitment of marriage, service and protection to each other, and sharing the possibility of new spirits in their children. The marriage is consummated at the height of this new couple's sexuality with complete open realms of spirituality, emotional openness, sexual and physical completeness and intellectual values, dancing in concert with each other.

As maturing follows young adulthood, the spirits of the adults grow and dance with determination to fulfill their dreams in choosing their own career, building their own home, having their own children as chosen by new spirits, establishing their own traditions, so alike, yet so different from all others in their chosen land. Many spirits

LOVE DANCES

soar in service to educate the young, healing the ill, farming the lands, working for the chosen people in private and public businesses, and building offices and homes to accommodate their jobs and families.

The dance of life realigns for the adult to further its spiritual possibilities. It realizes all it chooses to accomplish, for its family, its church of choice, its community, and travel to other lands throughout its world.

The dance of the owl wisely awakens to reign as partners to the adult. The lion offers strength of leadership with the commitment of courage. The chosen cats and dogs loyally serve to joyously offer merriment and protection to all. The other animals and critters each offer another special dance to the adult, sharing the vision of life's sound vibrations.

The soft inner spirit of the adult reaches comfort with its family and its things, no matter how sparse or abundant. The choice to serve others grows and the unconditional Love of the adult is set free to fly with the birds and bees creating a wonderful world of peace and harmony for all. This Love, so strong, conquers the pain and jealousies of other spirits seeking their own security

DANCING WITH ADULTS

through the insecurities of taking, rather than joyfully giving, as the rains of mother earth give that special gift of life for all to enjoy.

Dancing With Parents

The spirit of the adult chooses dances with other adults in its own special way. Spirits soar at a distance, then move in complete synchronization with another, seeking a soul mate to share in the ultimate energy exchange, the dance of birth, as all in the universe stands still for that split second when a spirit chooses and creates its chosen family in its world.

A child is born, with the blessings of God. The spirit is created within a child to its chosen parents in its chosen land. The dance of the child begins at the same moment that the dance of the parents begins.

The art and science, as far as that goes of parenting, begins with the birth of the child. The parents look to their own parents in their chosen land to determine the dance of parenting.

Some dances of parenting are tradition, some are experimental, some are limiting, while other steps are

DANCING WITH PARENTS

limitless. Other parental dances are painful, while other dances are pleasurable. The unconditional Love is always present no matter how soft, how strong, how naive or how illusive.

The greatest dance of all for a parent, is dancing the dance of an adult, with the freedom of a child, totally in concert with the desired steps and lessons for their child. As the parents choose to dance, as they desire the child to dance, Love is shared, encompassing all in creating the given behavior of this child, sometimes alike, yet, sometimes different. The parents and children dance together in loving bliss, sharing their lives with each other, their family and friends in their chosen land.

Some of the dances learned through the generations of the people in the chosen land, are old steps, the same for all, as are the traditions of the spirit's chosen people. Some children, with their unique qualities, while dancing with their parents and in their own space, begin to question and even rebel with new dance of life steps, different from the teachings of the elders.

The dance of the parent softly carries the inner spirits of the children through all in the chosen life; from their church of choice, to the selected schools for learning,

Love Dances

with family members in a small or large sharing of Love, into the community for the child to grow to adolescence and on to become an adult. They dance as their parents danced before them, sometimes to other lands with new steps, yet, retaining those special steps learned in their chosen family.

The adult dances as their parents danced, seeking a special partner to share life, whether married or in service to others, as one might choose a solo dance or a dance of partnership. Upon meeting and loving their chosen partner as a new adult, dances are shared with others, with the ever-changing rhythm in their newly and ongoing sharing of life's dances with each other.

The learned dances of the child, adolescent and adult are shared with friends and partners in the spirit's chosen land as parents danced the same dances when they were children, adolescents and adults. Steps may change as each spirit chooses its own destiny and its own life to be fulfilled with its own desires, yet, always retaining the fine thread of the same dance that was learned from its parents.

As one understands more fully the dance of their parents, rays of golden light are shared into one's life. In

Dancing With Parents

the same way the sunlight chases away darkness in the forest for the birds and animals to find life sustaining food and mates of their own kind to Love. They build a nest or find safety for the birth of their young in a clump of Aspen trees, creating new life for new spirits.

With each embrace of mother earth, growth is fostered for life sustaining and life creating dances to recreate oneself, as taught by the chosen parents, with only the soft changes of a given time in a given space by a given spirit in the chosen land.

Dancing With Grandparents

As your inner spirit softly and slowly changes from the primary role of parenting to that wonderful role of mentoring, loving and supporting all in one's chosen family as a grandparent, a most gracious dance occurs. The dance with grandparents maintains the strength for every family member from the newest child to the elderly aunts and uncles. Guidance, financial support and a home open to all is shared with unconditional Love, through the essence of God.

A time and place of healing occurs, where all can share and listen to each other as they cleanse, with Love, their questions about life and each dance that was chosen as well as the partners in those dances. Pain and guilt give way to a free audience of support as one dances with and as a grandparent.

The wonderful experiences of a lifetime embrace the grandparent as well as every other chosen elder in the family. The spirit continues to energize the continuance of the chosen people with every beautiful dawning, when the meadow larks, canaries and cocks give their special wake-up call with a melodious tune of life.

Grandparents dance to the early sounds, watering their rose, pansy and vegetable gardens supplying beauty and sustenance for their families and friends to enjoy. It is often a time for a grandparent to dance with a special hobby, tinkering with a car, chopping wood to fuel warmth to a home during the cold winter nights as snow softly blankets the earth or baking that special apple or cherry pie as the abundant fruit harvest is shared with all in the chosen land.

Sharing and caring are the dances of the grandparents, as they serve all in their chosen church, their political candidates of choice, their community and with any and all family members. Some contribute their learning of life at a job, to the future tillers of a family farm. Others teach children or young adults about life and its wonderful opportunities and choices.

As one's spirit chooses its destiny, a grandparent chooses to serve and support all from the birth of a new child, choosing its family, to the elderly, whether solo or

LOVE DANCES

encompassed by an extended family of children, grandchildren and as blessed by God, great grandchildren and great great grandchildren of one's chosen family.

As aging follows birth, grandparents assist and serve all. They dance with all family members sharing the inner courage to choose the dances of life and the dance to heaven as one's spirit leaves its special, revered place in the chosen land and its chosen people and all the wonderful experiences that it has enjoyed.

The dances with the spirits of the grandparents are the same, yet always changing and different. Science and discovery add new dimensions for a longer life and more time to serve others and to experience the enjoyment of those cherished moments with one's family at Christmas, religious celebrations or other special holidays. It is a time and place for that soft inner Love to be shared among all in one's chosen family and with all of its members.

The beauty, grace and dignity of the dances with grandparents soar as the soft clouds float endlessly in the sky, kissing the mountain tops with their tears of joy, sustaining the abundance of mother earth, for the growth of plants, trees and animals to dance and play among the forests, in a backyard or on a plain where life supporting plants and animals live in a soft balance.

These plants and animals serve others by sharing their lives for a new life. This is the same total Love and commitment that grandparents regally dance, while sharing with all their chosen family members in their chosen land.

Dancing With Your Family

As one's spirit, with the true essence of God, dances from childhood to heaven, a wonderful cast of chosen people support, guide and offer opportunities along life's special path chosen by this spirit. This gathering of people is referred to as one's family. It may be very small or include hundreds of chosen members with whom to dance.

The most special blessing is sharing unconditional Love with other family members in the chosen land. Families in the traditional sense, include parents and children of all ages; then add sisters and brothers dancing along through the years becoming aunts and uncles to serve and share their Love and understanding.

Adults become parents, parents become grandparents and the soft knitted connection of spirits flow from one dance to another almost without notice. Children grow to adolescence and on to become adults, dancing solo or

Dancing With Your Family

as a couple choosing a special mate, as they join in their unique minute when all stands still, intimately creating the opportunity for God and the universe to deliver a new blessed child.

One's chosen partner dances with the steps learned in their own special family, joining the dance of a new family sharing across blood lines without limits or restrictions. The Love soars as the celebration of life continues for this new couple, physically connected with the birth of their children, choosing this family. Others unite with their soul mates spiritually and emotionally without a chosen child, but always united with both families as one with children.

Another person or persons choose to dance openly with others outside the boundaries of the traditional family, accepting a child through adoption to join the new family totally. Others serve a mission of God with their own solo kind, bonding together in service for all the people in every chosen land, as a new family.

Sometimes, a family member, because of choice not in concert with the traditions of the family, may be expelled into the harshness of a new life, where they have the opportunity to dance with their own chosen lifestyle,

LOVE DANCES

whether solo as one dances with their own kind, with a prospective mate without the celebration of marriage, or as a married couple dancing a new and different life not accepted by tradition.

It is neither right nor wrong, it simply and completely serves the free spirit's choosing another choice to dance in the rays of new sunlight. Traditions and perceptions of the chosen people in the chosen land create homes and neighborhoods where all cannot live in peace and harmony because of the pain created by judgments, images and the what should be's.

Time heals all, as a family lets go of one member, though always softly connected. The person joins another chosen family weaving the new family as it is to be.

Peace and harmony are created again as the letting go under the true essence of Love, embraces and opens new doors for dancing in new churches of choice, to lifestyles different from those taught by the elders and politicians, and with different values and beliefs respecting all and allowing all their own choice of vision.

The flexibility of the family grows in strength, welcoming new members, unselfishly and without judgement, with the same beautiful gift as the fruit trees and dogwoods share their essence of colors, abundantly dancing across the land as the warm spring air chases away the coldness of winter.

The family blossoms as the trees and flowers blossom, bear fruit for all to enjoy and furnish a soft, protective haven for the blue birds and sparrows to build their nests for their own families, just as the chosen people in the chosen land choose their families.

Dancing With People From Other Lands

    *A*s the spirit chooses a dance among chosen people in a chosen land, it is open to the opportunity of dancing with all people throughout its universe. As the child begins its life, the spirit within, in the true essence of God, dances a unique quest of the chosen people, sharing and interacting with all others in its world, no matter how remote or far reaching.

    The soft inner spirit of the child knows no color, no religion, no creed or any other barrier to its complete openness and to the true unconditional Love it shares. It seeks this same Love from its chosen people.

    As it dances throughout its chosen land, it experiences beliefs from its chosen family, the church of its people, politicians of the land and all elders imprinting the beliefs and perpetuating limitations to the unconditional Love

Dancing With People From Other Lands

that the blessed child was born with, as it drew the first breaths of its life.

The traditions of the chosen people encourage, may even demand limitations or discrimination of one or another group of people from other races, religions, lands or whatever the differences might be from the chosen people. The spirits, finely connected by a silver thread, do not know the limitation of judgments or beliefs that any spirit in its chosen person is any different from any other being, no matter what land it lives in, what religion a person enjoys to worship, or the color of one's eyes or skin.

As one elephant in one land has certain physical attributes to survive through improved hearing or size, the same elephant in another land adapts physically as the rain forest demands differences in food and habitat from the savannahs. The spirits of these animals soar with each other, find their own mates of choice and share that special moment when all stands still as a new elephant is chosen and created to the chosen elephant in its chosen land.

The beautiful dance of life continues throughout all lands with wonderful, cultural differences, religious celebrations unique in their own way through their own chosen opportunities to worship God, and the founding of beliefs and states serving all of the people of each land well. People throughout time have physically and mentally changed gradually, as the pigmentation lightens or darkens and language and learning unite each other in each land to serve each inner spirit.

The beat and rhythms of each land pulsate the ambiance of a people, so graceful, so intricate and so free as all in a land celebrate birth, marriages, jobs and successes without limits, allowing all to be dancing the same dance, yet with individual steps in their own chosen way in each land. When people from one land begin to dance with people from another land, exchanges occur, some openly, some with reservation.

The people of different lands dance with exuberance, yet reservation, holding on to all that is sacred to them, as they exchange life and assimilate beliefs. People may develop or accept one common language. The soft inner spirit of each person, dancing with another person from another land, knows no difference in customs, beliefs, religions, physical differences or any other barriers or restrictions.

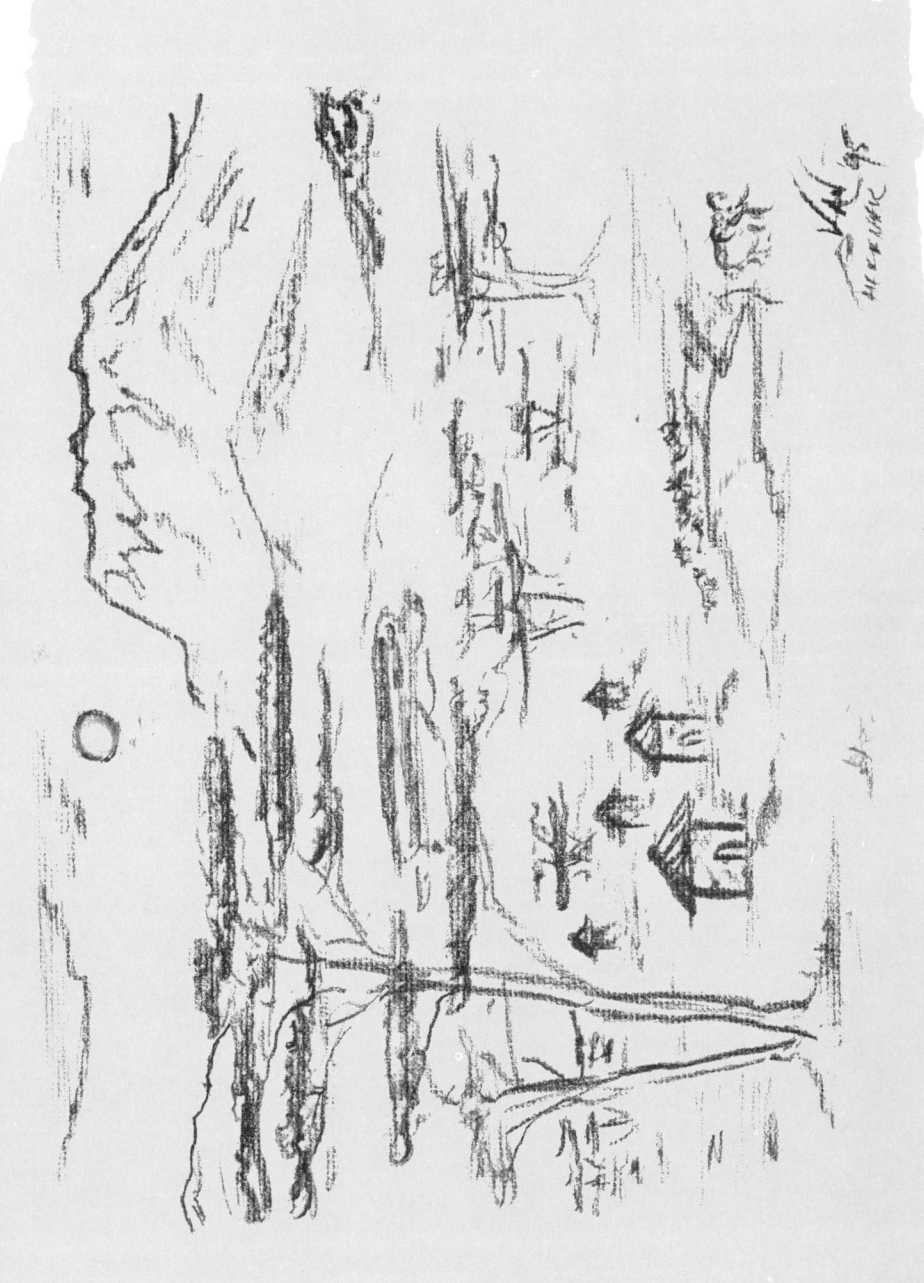

DANCING WITH PEOPLE FROM OTHER LANDS

Trust is built as one shares more and more without judgment, allowing all to dance their own steps with total acceptance and Love for all others dancing a different step, with unique adornments and physical attributes similar to all in each land, yet individual as one spirit is its own.

The world is a place for all people in every land to grow and learn as mother nature completes her cycle of providing food and special care for all. The daffodils and tulips are warmed by the early spring rays of life, growing, flowering and conserving its life in the earth for another season of salutation of beauty for all to enjoy.

The people of every land are warmed in the same way as the flowers of life, creating an inner strength and energy to unite all people. The spirits of one people, with the true essence of God, enjoy the dance of their life with all others. They dance as they have never danced before, with unconditional Love for all others in every land, creating total peace and harmony, with a passion for life for all in the universe.

Dancing With Music

The softly connecting voices of spirits ring from one chosen people to all the people of the universe through a realm of music. There are no boundaries or barriers for the universal language of Love through music touching each heart, in its own special way.

From the masterpieces of all time in the classical sense to a beautiful love ballad from the forests of Sherwood, an inspiring connection among all people occurs as each dances their own steps to the music of life, with a vision lifting each spirit in its essence of God.

As the child enters its life, so free and so alive, music surrounds the new spirit as the parents, elders and church congregations exude the sounds of the chosen land. The child dances with its individual beat, feeling the pulse of life, sciences and the arts of the people all around.

The child flows into adolescence with exuberance, to dance new steps with rhythms and rhymes making the statements of a new generation. The percussions and timbres of teenagers from one land transcends to all other lands, with only slight modulations, as youth dance the dances of adolescence.

The elders often respond in amazement, at what is happening in the now generations. They leave, momentarily their own youth, and soar with the dances of time, adamantly pronouncing the wall of aging, that their own youth was never like this.

Shocking as it may be, each generation of young people explodes onto the center stage of life, throwing all caution to the wind. They dance to the melodious sounds, or non melodious to some of the old folks, of their now generation, without any need to translate what feeling their new found sexuality and life is all about.

The youth dances into adulthood, retaining some steps to the music of memories. They learn new ones, both with the youth of tomorrow and the elders of yesterday.

One dances as its chosen people dances. They enjoy all of the dances from every other culture, as each spirit softly or vibrantly dances the heartbeat of life in each land.

Love Dances

Some music is so special that the soft inner spirit within one can feel the incredible beauty from generation to generation and from land to land in all the universe where life flourishes in its magnificence. The energy of this special music surrounds all in Love and creates the atmosphere where birds, animals and plants thrive as the people in the chosen land dance openly to wonderful sounds, through their inner spirits, their minds, in their hearts or on the ballroom floor of the grandest castle.

The classical sounds of one's culture continue the dance of a chosen people. They celebrate life in the salute or recognition of that special occasion for all in the chosen land.

The Love and forthcoming sexual intimacy of a couple, dance the dance of marriage, connecting melodiously each partner in commitment and inspiration for sharing ultimate Love. Energy stands still as the newly weds create that special moment, when their total Love brings forth joy as a new spirit chooses this special couple for its life as we know it.

Music is everywhere in the land. The birds share their voices in a chorus of mating, building their own nests and singing the song of food for their young.

Dancing With Music

The bears and bulls call to their mates with the passion of life, sometimes teasing, sometimes determined and sometimes without knowing anything else in their world is even happening. They dance with each other to the sounds of life, when all stands still, as new cubs and calves are created.

The sounds of mother nature caress all with the warnings of a brewing storm. After the drops of water, roars of thunder, and awakenings of lightning replenish the earth, the music of life continues for all. The birds, animals and people sing and dance in the radiance of another day, sparkling in the dew of the early morning, where all is full of Love and life.

Dancing With Art

*T*he vision of sharing a wonderful drawing, painting or sculpture with another, illuminates the young child with Love, blessed by the ever-growing God within this child. The spirits of young children dance a creative, free-flowing expression of color, design and value as they share their perceptions of their Love for their families, mother nature, anything or anyone in the chosen land.

At birth the spirit of the child is totally free of limitation to its creativity of what is and what is not art. They enjoy, unconditionally, the beautiful things around them as shared by their family and friends.

Parents, teachers in schools, leaders in their church of choice and elders of the community extend their judgments of life including perceptions of art upon the blessed child. As each year passes the inner spirit of the child, always present, transcends to a level of performing expectations and performing art as it is so interpreted by all in the chosen land.

Judgments about this free child create a dance of art in tradition not with the wonderful free creative spirit that is now so carefully masked. With each passing year, there is less and less creativity as the child passes into adolescence and on to adulthood, not willing to paint anymore elephants pink or mother nature's grass purple with the radiant orange sunsets of life.

Infrequently, a spirit within a special child, no matter what age in earthly years, chooses the dance of complete freedom, creating art to share with its world, no matter how vast or far-reaching. The spirit within this child remains free as the person ages.

The spirit dances with art in a kaleidoscope of colors and with medias, which no one has used before in its own unique way. This spirit captures the feelings within, expressing a complete Love in visions of life for all to enjoy.

As the composers combine all the notes and sounds of each instrument in their symphony, the artists create their dance of paintings and pieces illustrating their meaning and perceptions of life for their audience, magically portrayed for all time. The artists soar with inner passion

Love Dances

guiding the dance of art as they capture, for eternity, the new mother sharing the gift of life through her breast with her new child. This same child created only a short time ago when all stood still and the spirit connected with its chosen parents.

The Prussian blues of the sea, the snow capped peaks majestically framing the early morning sky, birds soaring, then diving for life as the Pelican seeks a fish for its meal, giving life to itself and its young, while setting free another spirit of a new life for another, this artist dances the vision of each special moment on one's canvass. Different strokes for different folks make art to one beautiful, while overlooked to another.

Dancing with art continues throughout life as surrealism, impressionism, and modern styles give way to tradition or era art representative of given people from a different land at a different time. Artists sometimes dance in colonies, infusing energy, technique and support with each other in the various centers of artistic learning. They dance in Florence, Paris, Bangkok, New York, San Francisco or one's own studio of life with chosen artistic friends.

The rapture of people caring for people, golden grain

DANCING WITH ART

waving the gift of food and life for all or an occurrence of hope, freedom and spiritual peace and harmony dance in the artist's soft inner spirit. The dance blossoms in a media of creative expression with total Love and acceptance of God. As one shares dancing with art with another, the inner spirit is filled with joy serving others with its same joy.

Dancing With Friends

*W*ith the first breath of life the spirit of the child dances in its special world of true Love, inspired by God. The chosen life of this child shares openly and completely with its parents in its chosen land. Soon other spirits of its family, friends and members of the chosen church gather in celebration of the remarkable happening, after all had stood still and a new baby was created.

The Love of this child dances from the start, seeking the return of the magical gift of Unconditional Love and nurturing from all of the people in the chosen land. As physical changes and growth occur, this spirit so finely connected to all others of its chosen families and people, develops verbal skills of language and physical communication attributes of non language, to reach out and touch the hearts of others in a beautiful way of acceptance.

The complete trust of this child is present encouraging

Dancing With Friends

openness and fun in seeking others outside of its chosen family to dance its dance of life. From a small child to the senior member of the chosen society, a special exuberance and high occur upon meeting another from another family or land.

From this first meeting of acquaintance, moments for dancing new steps with a new partner in a new way, move the relationship quickly from a fleeting eye contact of connection to one of friendship. The friendship between the two spirits of the chosen people soar to a level of confidence, trust, sharing and being as one, softly connected to the other by the fine purple thread of life.

Activities and memories tighten the budding friendship to the ultimate flowering of a commitment to life. This special friendship serves, as the pink rose buds blossom with mother nature, sharing their wonderful aromas, beauty and dignity for all of the chosen people to enjoy. The friends dance together in a special bliss of complete openness, sharing the pain and apprehensions of life, guiding each other through the rocks and rapids of life, expanding each other's world to new friends and experiences and enjoying each other in their unique way.

Without sexual intimacy, unless coupled in marriage

Love Dances

or another bond of commitment as defined in their own world in their own way, the friends dance throughout the land, sharing the wonderful foods, fashion and folderol that only true friends can create. They giggle, cry and embrace life to its fullest as the spirit of each person dances with passion the unconditional Love, peace and harmony with each other. Each so deftly demonstrates this Love for all to enjoy in their own universe.

Best friends, what a powerful dance of commitment and courage, serve each other. No matter how high the mountain top is to climb, how deep the valley is to farm, how swift the river flows to fish, or how vast the city is to see, they join together as partners, conquering all.

The Loving and caring bond, one to another of each friend, sometimes living out of the chosen land while visiting or working in another part of their world. They remain constant friends without jealousy, judgement or remorse, but always there for each other to dance with the same total acceptance, trust and vision when they reunite as when they last danced.

The ever-lasting dance of friends flows throughout life from birth to death and onto the kingdom of God in heaven serving each other with total Love and

DANCING WITH FRIENDS

acceptance. This bonding is real as the spirits of the Trumpeter Swan commits life to its mate in friendship, sharing birth of new swans when the pair stands still in that fleeting moment of time creating the spirit of a new swan. It swims its own quest of life, soaring beyond the marshes and tundras of the world onto the grainfields of abundance that mother nature and the farmers provide.

The swans call to each other in total harmony of life as a friend calls to another, dancing together in complete Love and harmony. That's what friends are for, for each other, forever.

Dancing With Feelings

The wonderful spirit within the newborn child surrounds itself with Love and contentment as it begins the journey of life. Passion soars from all as the spirits of the chosen people in the chosen land dance with their hearts, sharing joy to the new life, with the Love of God.

The blessed child experiences the first feelings at birth with an exacting mirror of all around. The feelings of a new mother, new father and seasoned grandparent connect spiritually with a fine yellow thread of life to the new baby. The feelings of joy, security, Love, nurturing and protection abound from all in the chosen family for the new one to quickly gain Love and acceptance from each member of its chosen family.

While totally open at birth the child soon learns to respond as the chosen family and elders of the community desire, starting a thin veil to the real feelings that are within the soft inner spirit of this child. As the years flow,

Dancing With Feelings

certain people cast a wonderful feeling along life's path as the child moves to adolescence and on to adulthood.

This chosen path glows with the openness of sharing each feeling, no matter how sensitive, how elating or how bold. Life beyond the path, may limit the demonstration of those inner feelings blocked with judgments of "shoulds" and "should nots." The freedom of expression of this person begins to experience a restriction or limit to the steps from its heart and begins dancing only those steps, taught by acceptance and learned from the chosen family, friends, church of choice and the politics of the land.

As the true feelings of this special spirit pull inside, the child begins building walls to its heart, carrying these along its way limiting its freedom, as the forest limits the growth of trees that are leaning on each other or crowded together without the ability to grow straight and tall in the magic of a day's sunlight. Walls are removed only by risking, including rejection, fear of failure, condemnations and all the other feelings creating a life of threat and insecurity.

Sharing the inner feelings through Love and honesty create total trust and harmony within and among all of the

Love Dances

chosen people. The dance of total acceptance and complete freedom casts its magical spell on all who are touched by it.

Complete Love and caring is shared as couples dance still during that special moment when life is chosen and is again created for each new spirit. Families dance wildly with children running hither and yon.

Grandparents dance graciously through assisting all in their lives and to the heavens for each. The community and state dance with new unrestricted beats as the church and political leaders respond openly and honestly, leaving the perceptions of what others think and what is tradition, behind.

The spirits of all soar in an ambiance so regal that each yellow ray dances and caresses the inner soul of life creating unconditional Love for all in a universe of peace and harmony. Mother nature shares her beauty and her heart, creating a reflection of every plant, animal and bird.

As the magpie jealously guards its trinkets and treasures in its nest, the doves share Love for all in expressing the coos of peace. The magpies of the world squawk a dance filled with deception and scavengering, while the doves radiate acceptance dancing with all partners including their adversaries. They empower the world with complete trust and harmony.

When each spirit dances the dance of complete honesty of heart, every spirit connects in total Love and harmony, comfortably removing all walls, no matter how small or how large. Passion and freedom are shared for every spirit in every chosen person as the feelings of Love are created and shared heart to heart, as the soft connection of each fine yellow ribbon continues the spiritual lifeline between a new child and its chosen family.

Dancing With Dating

Shortly after the spirit of the child enters its chosen family, it openly observes the dances of relationships all around it. The blessed child's parents present the message of Love, caring and tenderness to the child. The God within one grows with Love, as all other relationships are experienced by the growing child.

The safety of a dance for a child with one's own sex establishes special playmates and buddies to play and enjoy life only as the free spirits of children can dance. The teachings of parents, elders from the church of choice, school teachers and principals imprint the expected beliefs for this special child and its friends.

The guidance of all in the chosen land establishes the accepted dances and foreign steps for the children and early adolescents. As children physically grow and change during puberty, the energy shifts in a unique, yet sometimes frightening way. They leave the safety of their

Dancing With Dating

own sex and begin to dance the flirtatious dances of attracting others as they each try the dance of dating.

Their new found sexuality fuels an inner flame brightly glowing for their old pals and playmates, as well as attracting new ones. Often, new same sex friends group together in a dance of attracting their targets of attention. The gyrations heighten as the opposite sex targets respond from their own new group pals or playmates, dancing onto that special floor of a first touch, a soft kiss or a hug, where bodies meet, but not totally letting go of the safety of one's physical space.

The dances change, the rhythms flow, then pulsate, as the teenager soars with one's own spirit softly connected by a lavender thread to other spirits of adolescents or youths. Mother nature shares the same gift of lavender in the lilacs with their captivating aroma of life, enticing birds, bees and all Lovers. They may share a walk in the radiance of springtime or passionate Love with complete oneness, when all stands still during that special moment when two become one and a new spirit arrives, if so chosen, to all beings.

Each person dances to their own shining star, twinkling and strutting their stuff for one or all in the

Love Dances

chosen land to enjoy. The dating dances continue with spirits changing partners as the rhythms of life change. They search and seek the final connection with the chosen spirit of their ultimate soul mate.

The dating continues throughout the spirit's chosen life, never fading, always glowing, checking each other out. Upon finding the ultimate soul mate, blessed by God in heaven, they continue that special dance with the chosen spirit connected so perfectly with one another that true unconditional Love bonds them together creating complete peace and harmony. This dance, the dance of dating, is danced throughout every land, by every being in the universe.

Mother nature assures the continuance of life and Love for all the plants, animals and birds, as each serves another in the arena of the forests, the meadows or on the mountain tops. The mountain sheep crack heads, butting their stuff with each other.

The wild mustangs dance the dating dance, kicking and nipping each other. The ruffled grouse puffs his chest the same as the man puffs his on the beach of choice, enticing beautiful girls in their bikinis, just as the grouse to a hen.

DANCING WITH DATING

The winds of dating encompass all. The dating dance flirts and soars here and there as each kind seeks its special partner to dance as only they can dance.

Dancing from their hearts with the total passion of life and Love, each spirit finds its own partner. Sometimes so alike and sometimes so opposite. They live together in their chosen way with Love, peace and complete harmony.

Dancing With Marriage

As the spirits within youth and adults alike dance with ever-changing dates, often one special connection is chosen, as blessed by God. This special being is chosen with total Love, care and acceptance for all that this spirit is and all that this spirit is not.

Sometimes opposite, sometimes exacting a mirror of oneself, the person commits a permanency as established by the traditions of the people in the chosen land. No matter what way, what religious beliefs or political law bonds one to another in matrimony, marriage offers that total commitment of Love and life for the inner spirits to dance as two beings connected so gently, yet so passionately, by the beautiful red thread of marriage.

The vibrancy of the red thread connects one heart to another sharing Love unconditionally, in peace, security and harmony when one finds one's soul mate in its own universe. The red thread spiritually unites two into one,

DANCING WITH MARRIAGE

when all stands still and the gift of life is blessed by God as a new spirit chooses its parents, if the time is so chosen, uniting the blood of each other into this special baby.

The dance of marriage is wonderfully different throughout all of the lands. Sometimes arranged by the elders of a chosen people, they determine in their own thoughts, whom should dance the dance of marriage and procreation with whom, often without question or without heart. Some spiritually soar together in bliss as if chosen by one's own spirit which had actually happened anyway, while others live the tradition as the tradition is to be lived.

The spirits of people in other lands dance the dance of courting and marriage as the traditions of those people and beings choose to dance. Sometimes accomplishing life threatening deeds, a young man may choose his bride as recognition of this honor.

A family in one land may give cows or goats to create a dance of marriage for their son or daughter. Others marry only of their own social status, from royalty to royalty or caste to caste, established by tradition, yet so chosen by each inner spirit.

LOVE DANCES

The dance with marriage is as each spirit softly and gently chooses its dance. Some are totally Loving, some passionately fueled in sexual intimacy, exploding to heights of unbelievability. Others are bonded for closest friendship. Some connect with lessons of conflict or opposing judgments, limiting all other levels of closeness.

Each special marriage dances steps of tradition. New steps of exploratory rhythms create life in a new way. These are beats of passion and beats of Love, beats of comfort and notes to sing as joy fills the beautiful relationship called marriage.

Some choose a solo marriage, not with a partner but with God in service to one's church of choice and its house of service to all the people in every land. Other solo marriages are in spirit only, not in the traditional sense, but with a heart of commitment to one's family or a spiritual connection with one's own mirror image in another spirit.

Mother nature offers the dance of marriage to each spirit of all plants, animals, birds and fish. Sometimes the marriage is only for a split second. A second when all stands still in the universe and the brook trouts share their eggs and meld creating new roe, fertilized with the gift of

DANCING WITH MARRIAGE

new spirits energizing fish for all its streams of choice.

The blossoms of life abound in the marriage of male and female flowers of trees and plants. They surround all in nature with captivating aromas attracting bees, birds and animals to assist with fertilization for that split second when all stands still in the marriage of the pollens, creating the fruits and seeds of a new tree, bush or plant.

One spirit's allergy is another spirit's gift of marriage and blessed life in a dance so grand, yet so subtle, that all sing the chorus of birth and new beings in this unique life. The balance is fine, and every spirit shares with mother earth the abundance to sustain a wonderful life of Love, peace and harmony for all living things.

Dancing With Learning

*T*he dance of learning begins as the blessed child starts an incredible life and continues until the spirit chooses to travel home to its heaven. All is shared with the new baby as it observes, listens, tests and responds to everyone in its chosen family and with everyone it meets.

The leaders and elders in the chosen land teach the steps of learning, formally through educational programs, set in place by the traditions of the schools, the church of choice and the politicians of the land. The times to go, and the times to stay, are guides to the small child as it follows the path chosen by the inner spirit so softly and delicately balanced to learn all.

The child learns quickly to communicate with sounds and motions to assure nurturing, Love and all it chooses to mirror from the lives of the chosen people. The child receives the reflection of desired lessons from its parents, family, friends and all in the community.

Dancing With Learning

The free flowing absorption of knowledge sometimes slows down or detours with judgments, expectations and only certain acceptable traditions from the leaders and elders in the community. All are part of the special dance of learning.

The parents and family are the brightest guiding stars. The educators and church leaders are next, with traditions and values of choice. Lastly, the politicians implement and change the learning laws of the land.

The power of words, no matter what language or languages are in the chosen land, impact the blessed child, inspired and guided by God, imprint the learning process so strongly and so enabling that the course of a life is formed in the first few years. The capacity of learning is softly and intricately present. All which enhances this openness cast unlimited opportunities as the spirit chooses its dance of knowledge.

Traditions of learning, sometimes only consider the process to occur at a given place, given time, with given leaders and elders, are set, yet are changing as the spirits change in interaction to all others. The spirits of the leaders and elders choose their dance of teaching and learning for others according to their own perceptions

LOVE DANCES

and traditions. At a certain age in a land, the children and young people show up to be taught the lessons of the spirit's chosen people.

The ludicrous lesson lies in thinking that this is now the time for learning to take place, and the other time is dedicated to other activities without learning. Traditions and judgments are so funny.

Spirits dance with learning from the first breath of life. The most important teachers can be the parents and family of the blessed child, sharing a beautiful fine thread of learning with the teachers at the schools, the church elders and all others in the chosen land.

The dance of learning weaves and spins with all in the spirit's chosen life, with parents, mates, grandparents, children and all other spirits in our chosen land, as well as, all other lands in the universe, as we travel and work. The sharing, caring and learning serve the opportunity for new steps of knowledge.

Unconditional Love between two partners, as shared in a way of learning, is expressed totally as the hearts connect for that split second when all stands still and a new spirit can choose a new life with its chosen parents. These same learned ways of all the beings in mother

Dancing With Learning

nature share the dance of learning as taught from others. Sometimes these lessons are self taught when all soar together, as the swallows fly free on the first days of summer building a nest to house its young under the eaves of a church or bridge spanning a magnificent river.

The learning of the chosen people dances between all people, with the animals and birds of the land and with mother nature sharing her abundance of life and minerals. The careful balance, so softly connected, offers learning for all and an opportunity to reap knowledge and sustenance as one sews its seeds of life in every way.

Dancing With Money

Choices of the new spirit in the child are varied and vast as one envisions its life and its wonderful path filled with unique experiences that only this chosen person dances. One part of that life, that might be so abundant for one, and so sparse for another, is purely seen in the eyes of the chosen. It dances with money.

Money represents a universe of variety to people in every land. From power, prestige and fame to a simple meal for the loved ones in a chosen family, the dance with money is the creation of choice for the spirit within that newborn child when all stood still and it chose its special family.

As the spirit dances through its life, one stage changes to another, from childhood, to adolescence, adulthood, parenthood, grandparenthood and on to its heaven of choice. The lifestyle is there, so softly, yet so fluid and dynamic as some doors are closed, new doors open for new opportunities, assisting all to learn its dance steps of money.

At a young age, the parents, teachers, elders, church leaders and politicians share and often direct the dance of a career or job for the spirit within the growing child. This choice becomes money, or appears as a vehicle to earn money, as one dances in the trenches, operating rooms or with mother earth to create that special lifestyle as it is to be for the chosen one.

The true inner spirit, with the essence of God, knows its mission of service of sharing unconditional Love, peace and harmony for all. This often is layered with the things money can and cannot buy, as are the traditions of the people in the chosen land. The cars, the clothes, the sticks and bricks we call our homes all mean something to the people in the chosen land, sometimes the same status of success, sometimes a statement of selfishness and greed.

The dance of money is a dance of attitude, as one has and one has not, or an open, beautiful dance of sharing Love and one's abundance with those who can be served by this abundance. The dance is one of equality not a dance of doing for doing's sake.

Love Dances

The inner spirits of all know the open dance of complete sharing and appreciation of the money of each, no matter what it looks like. When people remove the facades of the traditions about the amount of money a person has, how one dresses, looks or is sheltered, a miracle of lifestyle occurs for the inner being to dance with money through complete Love having the true heartbeat of life.

As in mother nature, the majestic bull elk, dances with its money of possessing so many cows that it cannot protect or serve each in that special moment, when all stands still as it couples with a chosen cow at a special moment, when a new spirit chooses to be a new calf in the meadow and mountains of its chosen herd. Another bull elk may choose to share its life with only one special cow with so much abundance of Love that as it stands still in that blissful moment and a new elk is created, a humble and beautiful lifestyle is chosen. This small family has complete Love, abundance and safety in its small band.

Just as in the majestic mountains or on the flower-carpeted meadows of the land of Elk, people choose their dance of money with themselves, their families and with

DANCING WITH MONEY

all in the chosen land. The dance never is as it looks to others.

One must go inside to the inner spirit, knowing the gift of freedom from all worries, hunger or pestilence. A bowl of rice, with a small minnow is the same as the filet with its Bernaise sauce and baked potato smothered in the abundant creams of choice in a different life, when shared with unconditional Love and caring for each other in the chosen land.

Dancing With Fun

Joy comes naturally to the new born spirit in a child so exuberant with all its surroundings. It laughs and cries dancing its fun and lack of fun with its parents, friends and everything in the chosen land.

As one ages along the chosen path of life, the inner spirit creates and dances new steps of fun, with its true essence of God. The child grows and radiates one activity, possibly solo, then shared with a friend or two, then on to a whole classroom of buddies. The beat changes and shifts to wonderful dances of flirtation with adolescent girls and boys gyrating their stuff for themselves, their buddies and most of all, their opposite attractions.

Fun is the universal joy for all with Love so strong, that cares fly away with the wind of time. The bright yellow threads of the inner spirits softly connect all in their meaning of fun, sometimes so alike, sometimes so

Dancing With Fun

different, for each spirit in the chosen land.

Life is filled with fun, from the inner joy, romance and intrigue, so captivatingly written in the words of a book, to a championship ball game when the entire community or state magnetically supports its athletes in celebration of playing and winning the big game. Dancing with fun soars with no limits for Love.

Ultimate romance is shared between two beings when all stands still in the universe. Joy reigns at this split second when a new spirit has the opportunity to join a family in its own time and its own way.

The passages of time in one's life create opportunities for small children to enjoy the fun of sifting sand through their fingers, creating that special freedom of motion for everything. Hobbies for youth and grandparents alike connect each to another, while fishing for a catfish on a lazy summer day along the bayou. Sharing the dance of fun and joy with each other, they pass the traditions of the elder spirits to the inquisitive leaders of tomorrow in the chosen land.

Just as the hyena laughs its story about life, food and Love to each one of its pups on the rifts of its world, the salamander focuses its wriggles in a dance of fun with one

LOVE DANCES

another in the cool, clear pool nestled with crisp watercress furnishing food, protection and a birth place for the spirits of new salamanders. They choose life in this chosen place, when all stands still for that explosive second of that special pairing of life.

The chosen land enraptures joy for all as the dance of fun connects everyone and everything in their own special way. The baking of a sour cream chocolate cake covered with shimmering frosting by a grandparent, tempts all who pass its captivating appearance and aroma.

A quick finger of a youth's inner spirit, no matter what age, dances in fun as a connection is made, uniting a finger, the frosting of the delicious cake and the watering mouth of pleasure. Grandma raises an arched eyebrow of disapproval, then grabs grandpa and dances in the radiance of fun, hugging and kissing the little boy, so much alive in the old fool.

The dance of fun is all around. The birds chase each other through the trees. The bees pollinate every flower, dancing the dance of the bumble bee. The dogs bark and wag their tails in joy, welcoming every family member home.

The inner spirit of every being dances in their own

Dancing With Fun

special way through out its chosen life and on to the ultimate grand ballroom in its heaven with all its Loved ones. The spirits abound in the yellow rays of fun, sharing one with oneself, each other, and every living plant, person and thing in total Love, peace and harmony throughout its chosen universe for eternity.

Dancing With Dogs, Cats & Roses

The soft affectionate kiss of a puppy connects, ever so gently, with the new spirit of the blessed child toddling along. A fluffy kitten snuggles next to the sleeping baby, purring their Love with each other.

The radiant aroma from the gardens encompass the blessed child in the full essence of God, as the new spirit explores life among the roses, petunias, nasturtiums and tulips. Each colorful flower casts its show, to fulfill and complete the kaleidoscope of colors, welcoming all to the homes of the chosen people.

The dance of the chosen people with their pets, and in their gardens, extends each spirit of every being with warmth, understanding and complete unconditional Love for all. From the young child playing with her dog, the teasing game between a cat and a small boy and gardens for all to cultivate life providing vegetables, herbs, and flowers, add sparkles of joy to the dances.

When the spirit of the chosen person is tired, discouraged or feeling down and troubled, the blessed spirit, in the true essence of God, in every pet responds with unconditional Love as the song of each canary trills its excitement, welcome and security to all. The gold and tropical fish greet all comers with a wriggle and a kiss against the glass of their world, dancing exuberance at being fed a flake of sustenance from its chosen person.

From a spiritually moving day with one's church members, to challenges from one's boss, or that special time with an elder dancing in the twilight of retirement, one enters that sacred reunion with mother nature in the gardens of the ground earth in the chosen land. The dance of freedom soars to new heights as one tills the soil and plants seeds creating new life for every vegetable and flower. Then it is harvest time of bountiful crops, as the plants and flowers share their special dance of life with all of the chosen family and friends.

Peace and harmony reign in the gardens. All pressures and emotional pain fly away with the beautiful scents of the gardens.

Love Dances

The child within plays in the gardens no matter how intimate or vast. Life's wonderful cycle continues with the dance, when all stands still for a split second, and a spirit chooses new life as a child, a new bird, a new sweet basil plant or cosmos, electrifying the summer days with its fluorescence, fertilized by the bees and insects of its life.

Serving the spirit within the chosen person, from the youngest to the most senior, the dances caress the inner spirit with the dogs, cats and roses of their lives in the fullest and complete steps of unity. The dance flows wistfully as the sun stimulates the growth of all. The flash of lightning, with its resonating thunder, adds life giving cleansing of the air for the leaves of all to stretch upward, in new ways, with the energy within everyone and everything in the gardens.

The tunes of the home change the energy of each house plant as well as the pets singing and purring the contentments of their chosen homes. The chosen family dances with food, playfulness, unconditional Love and acceptance, for and from each pet and plant, with which the chosen people surround themselves in their chosen land.

Dancing With Dogs, Cats & Roses

The moon welcomes the exchange of the oxygens and carbons of the contribution of new vapors dancing along the silver beam in the nights of their lives. The first rays of dawn call the bantam cocks to crow the awakenings of each spirit to the radiance, created for the here and now in all its glory.

The bantam cock struts his dance of seduction for any bantam hen who might be interested in coupling in the still of the dawn, creating that breathless moment when all stands still. The egg within is fertilized for the new chick to be hatched by its chosen mother from its nest of life, under the spiraea in the garden.

From our traditional pets and plants to the most unique ones, the child within chooses its family, its pets and plants as they choose the chosen people dancing with each other in total radiance and acceptance. Pets and gardens change as the spirits of the chosen people softly and Lovingly move along the chosen path of destiny. They fly freely from the chosen land to the kingdom of heaven, where all live together in peace, harmony and Love for eternity.

Dancing With Birds, Bears, Trees, Mountains & Streams

At the split second when a new spirit chooses its life, it surrounds itself with mother nature and her natural beauty in the world chosen. The cascading streams cast diamonds from the mountains, majestically embracing the ever-changing skies, to the fertile valleys caressing life in all plants and animals sharing with the chosen people.

The magical changes of the seasons create ever-changing dances in the birds soaring north or south to their nesting places. They create new terns and ducklings, when all stands still in the universe for a split second and a new Arctic tern or mallard duckling chooses its path of life

The plants and trees join the dance of the seasons. Blossoming in only the way they each may blossom, they

DANCING WITH BIRDS, BEARS, TREES, MOUNTAINS & STREAMS

share total Love through the pollens and fruits of creating new plants and trees, as all stands still for the split second, as new life is created.

The world is a totally beautiful place, with soft interconnecting energy basking in the golden rays of sunlight by day, crystal droplets of rain and dew sharing the drinks of life for all. The vermillions of all the plants and trees replenish the air that all the chosen breath, even though they rarely acknowledge mother nature for this gift of life. Each spirit of every being is welcomed by mother nature to dance in their own way, in their own land.

Caution is shared to each spirit within. Enjoy the special gift of life that is created for every being, in the true essence of God.

Protect and do not abuse this environment where all people, birds and bears dance in their own way, in their chosen forest of life. The balance of life and death is sacred, too much or too little harvesting of the trees casts the doom of death to the forest, no matter how extensive the forest might be or even for a solo tree in one's backyard.

Love Dances

A forest unattended and not harvested naturally, becomes over grown with underbrush and diseased trees. It loses supporting space for each tree and plant to grow in its own radiant sunlight.

The forest may fall victim to mother nature's natural recycling of all, when the summer thunder and lightning storm ignites the stressed and diseased trees, burning all. This leaves only a few seeds from the winds of time to replenish the green aura of life, for the birds and bears, that danced among the leaves of their chosen forest, only a few days before with their babies.

When the intrusion of people in the chosen land dance with judgment and restriction, the forest, too, becomes prey to destruction. Caution is shared with the dance of extremes. Too much harvest or no harvest, each will create death in its own way to the forest.

Proper harvesting, not stripping and bludgeoning of all in the forest, allows the removal of tired and diseased trees, and underbrush smothered by forest weaknesses. This opens up vistas of life for strong, beautiful trees and numerous nesting places for the chosen owls of its chosen forest.

The spirits of the birds, bears and trees in the chosen

Dancing With Birds, Bears, Trees, Mountains & Streams

land dance with the spirits of every person in the chosen land. The beat of harmony and unconditional Love reigns for all as the people allow the berries of the mountains and salmons in the stream to furnish the ongoing gift of life to the cinnamon bear.

The bear's freedom abounds in its natural habitat, where it growls the dance of Love with its mate for a split second, as all in its universe stands still. A new spirit of life can choose its dance as a cinnamon bear cub enjoying the ever-changing huckleberry patches and gourmet chinook salmon in the autumn of its childhood.

Life for all on the planet soars unconditionally, as the fine thread of balance is softly connected with respect for each other; then dancing loosely and with ever-changing steps as each spirit serves every bird, bear, tree, mountain and stream, sustaining and protecting life. The spirits dance in the green and platinum light of goodness for every living thing, creating Love, peace and harmony for the chosen people in its chosen world for eternity.

Dancing With Courage & Risk

The chosen spirit's journey through its life is filled with its own special opportunity to dance as only it might dance. As each day furnishes challenges of new people and things, the spirit within the small child, in the true essence of God, makes choices in interactions with all in the chosen land.

The guiding traditions of the child's parents and family, elders of the church of choice, politicians of the state and community leaders impact the spirit within, sometimes softly, sometimes boldly. The child learns the dance steps of conformity, compliance and sometimes rebellion in search of inner feelings of comfort and security.

What the child or adolescent wants, changes as all in its world changes with each whim and new moment. One lesson learned from the first day of life is that the new baby's cry may experience the feeling of total Love,

Dancing With Courage & Risk

acceptance and approval, while another spirit within another small child may have chosen a different dance with its chosen family.

One spirit's strife may be another spirit's smooth stride down its racetrack of its chosen life. The child, adolescent and young adult dance with courage and risk for unconditional Love, acceptance and whatever it feels turns it on, vibrating and moving as only it chooses to move with its family, friends and others.

When the traditions of the land are questioned, the spirit within the chosen person knows the mission and vision of meaning in its life. As one grows and changes, often in concert with the dance of its family and community, a person leaves its comfort zone and stands up for the dance it wants to dance.

The risk is frightening, sometimes intimidating but true. The stretch for growth, acceptance and freedom builds the admirable choices as the person goes along its chosen path.

The young adult chooses a Love dance with its mate, or a dance solo, sometimes alone, sometimes with one in its mirror of its comfort essence. The beauty of the blessed couple, committing courage to a marriage in the

Love Dances

tradition of its chosen land, share Love in that special way for that explosive second when all in its universe stands still. The wonderful risk is total, open and free for a new spirit to choose its family and its own life in its own way.

The courage for others grows as one solo dancer, serves the church of choice, committed to serve all others unconditionally, in its community, with its family or special friends. The risk of judgment by the elders and leaders of the chosen land sometimes ignorantly, sometimes with severe condemnation, shines through with the radiance of courage. One chooses its own dance of life, sometimes marrying a person from another religion, culture or land, sometimes choosing not to marry but serving and building its own life and home as it chooses.

The courage of life is that same courage that mother nature shares. The prairie dog whistles for a mate in the closing weeks of winter, as Love and passion stir its mating call to a melodious tune, that even the coyote waiting for a dinner with the prairie dog is caught off guard by the piper's style and boldness. The tawny dog dances with complete risk and courage out of her hole to check out the dance of her future mate. The two soar

Dancing With Courage & Risk

with total bliss, coupling during that split second when all stands still and new prairie pups choose the beautiful life in its own Kansas.

Dancing with risk and courage transforms the spirit within the chosen person to complete freedom, harmony and peace in its own family. Love soars and is reflected back as one risks with another.

One may experience a wall or roadblock, only to step aside without judgment, but, with complete acceptance for another spirit within a person at a different space in time. One success of courage follows another, as the spirit within is released and is softly connected with all beings in its chosen land.

The path is comfortable, as one can agree, disagree, be oneself and respecting each other totally, without limits or judgments. One achieves the unconditional Love that is created for eternity through its spirit's courage.

Dancing With Care

When parents choose the opportunity for a new child to be born, they embrace total Love, with the true essence of God, for this child. As the first earthly breath is drawn by the chosen child, the dance of care comes unconditionally from the parents, family and people in the chosen land.

Care for this tender spirit is all encompassing, from the physical sustenance, to clothing, shelter, warmth or coolness as the needs might be. Far beyond the physical needs are spiritual, emotional, intellectual and social needs, often in concert with the traditions of the chosen land.

Dancing with care is that inner spiritual feeling, which one has for another, sometimes empathetic and other times sympathetic feelings. The heart to heart connection is so soft, yet so strong, that when one feels sorrow or grief, another spirit, dancing with care, can give total

Dancing With Care

Love and support during the difficult time, allowing complete independence of the other to a song of empathy.

When a heart connects to another heart with the same pain, joy or exultation, the spirits dance together in the aura of a sympathetic tune both unconditionally feeling the same pain, passion or angelicness of the moment. The care shared on the same dance floor, becomes synchronized as the synchronized swimmers perform, as the geese on the lakes float together toward the nest of life where all stands still and a new gosling has chosen its family to swim with the same imprint.

Neither connection is right or wrong, it is only the dance of the moment, as a mother comforts her small child after a roller blading skinned knee, or an aging grandparent assists their loved ones home to their heaven of choice. Dancing with care changes as the spirits within make a new choice with their partners, from a dance of empathy to a dance of sympathy and back again.

The feelings within the all knowing spirit of a person, plant or animal, are caressed as mother nature caresses with care the lands of time, no matter how barren as the parched deserts or the fertile valleys of the world, like the Nile River flowing as the longest river sharing its gift of

Love Dances

life to all people along its banks throughout time.

The care of a great ruler creates pyramids of transition to its heaven as the temple saluting a life and the people of its time. These dances with care about the people, animals, jewels and things of the times, become for generations following, creative, archeological history and culture.

The same care is within the family floating among the reeds along the banks of the Nile, catching fish for their dinner, grains for their breads and to feed a Nubian goat or two. Each dance with care is connected gently with the other, as each spirit within different people is connected to do theirs, dancing with the most complex life to the simplest one of survival.

Love is shared by all the spirits in the land, whether the pharaoh coupling with his queen from the palace of his kingdom, or the peasant finding a bride so caring that their connection is so total. All stands still and one new spirit chooses to be a future Ramses and another spirit chooses to be closest to mother earth with her fish, grains and goats.

Both new children dance in different homes, yet totally share the same spiritual connection. These dances

Dancing With Care

of care are filled with unconditional Love, empathy and sympathy from their chosen families and people in their community of choice and being.

The seasons in the chosen lands change one to another, as the spirit's chosen life and the lessons flow along, as the Nile River flows to its destiny. The support of each spirit's family soars as the Ibis seeks its grains and river creatures of life to feed its family. The great white birds, so graceful, so beautiful, care for each other with the calls of Love for mating, food or its young, dancing with care for all to enjoy the gift to each other.

The family members dance in the same way with each other. They dance with complete care, without the limits of judgment or what ifs, changing as the meanings of the spirits within change.

Dancing with care serves all. Sometimes the dance is sympathetic, sometimes empathetic, but always with unconditional Love, creating peace and harmony for each spirit in every person, in one's home, in the chosen land and on to its heaven.

Dancing With Judgments & Nerds

The traditions of the chosen people are shared with each new person as the spirit within chooses its family and its community. Beliefs of the politicians of the land, the church leaders, elders and senior family members set the values, cultural attitudes and acceptable behaviors for all.

From day one, the dance at birth begins with the chosen people sharing traditions, blessings of the God within and even the way Love is shared or withheld. What is judged by others, as the right and wrong ways for the people in the chosen land, gives way to the acceptable dance steps for each year as the young child matures along life's path.

Where to live, what to do, who to be with, and who not to be with, shape the beliefs of each society in its own

Dancing With Judgments & Nerds

way. The soft inner spirit knows what is true for it, but soon the child places small bricks around it, as walls of judgment are built around the inner self.

The child seeks approval and acceptance from each interaction with its family, friends, church members and the community. It begins to mirror what is expected, not what is always known in its heart. Children are wonderfully honest and open at birth, then begin to close themselves off behind the walls of judgment, to avoid rejection, castigation or other painful reactions when one searches for the real truth, in lieu of what is expected.

The soft inner voice within, always knows the truth differing at times from the strong debates of rights and wrongs taught by others. Each spirit within every being has a wonderful personality, even when it dances with the judgments of others.

This nerd dance stumbles and bumps through life in a funny interaction with all, presenting the nerd self to everyone in the chosen land. The nerds in all of us, at times all too serious, present what is the judgmental traditions, perfection and the way we are suppose to act among the chosen people.

Some spirits mask their inner being through analysis,

LOVE DANCES

reasoning why there is air, while others, impressionistic and superficial, say flippantly, I care. Another person learns to manipulate and control others, while being out of the game of life before they were in it.

The dances go on and on to the stages of life. Dramatically, the poor victims and martyrs weep and whine to get their way, only to send loved ones far away.

What a hoot these ways of life become, as the owls in the forest or on the farm, know what is and what is not. Mother nature does not care about the impressions of that great bird, only the inner spirit of sharing Love and life with its partner, when all stands still and new baby owls choose the life in the forest or in the barnyards of their new world.

The dance of judgments serves only to restrict or block rigidly, the spirit within each of the chosen people. As the dance continues and becomes tradition, the spirits within each person are masked with funny faces, contorted bodies, make-up and hairdo's that any Nerd would be proud of in the hilarious kingdom of Nerdom.

The inner spirits know the incredible power of openness and flexibility. Being in your heart, without judgment, and totally accepting of others with unconditional Love and caring, creates peace and harmony within each person and throughout all people in the world for eternity.

Dancing With Joy & Magnificence

The soft inner spirit within every person in the chosen land has an unbelievable quality of magnificence, creating joy for the person and every family member and friend. This radiance beams with many different rays on a magnificent dance floor of life so captivating, charming and intoxicating that all want to experience the inner joy and contentment with this partner.

Just as the nerd within a person can drive others crazy, the joy in another creates an open and inviting connection for all others with the true essence of God. The spirit's joy and magnificence dances with knowing steps in the chosen land, attracting all others to its side for a wonderful exchange of total Love and happiness.

Each person's joy and magnificence are unique and special in one's own way. The inner spirit from the heart shares unconditionally and keeps giving and giving with fun, excitement and in so many Loving ways.

The inner spirit of a person in one's magnificence exerts the powerful freedoms of being, yet with the softness, gentleness and caring as only grandparents care for their own children and grandchildren.

When a macho nerd is transformed from a seductive, controlling, judgmental, all too cool dude, into his true magnificence, he shines brilliantly as a beautiful man, dancing with gentleness, honesty, Love and himself. He then dances with care in this magnificence with the beautiful women and all the special people in his life.

An unbelievable renaissance occurs and the truly beautiful man becomes real with the true spirit of magnificence inside, letting go of the insecurity of his image. As the nerd of the macho man is dissolved, so can the nerdiness of the flirtatious, painted-up, rolled and curled, tinted-haired woman playing the same, yet different, game of searching for that soft, feminine identity.

This image masks, oh so colorfully, her desired game searching to quell the insecurity of rejection from the males, she so desperately attempts to attract. As she

Love Dances

becomes real, she lets go of her image. The soft inner beauty soars on her special dance floor, with acceptance of herself and her special femininity, then sharing magnificently with the women, children and finally the men in her life.

The joy radiates from within this woman. Her spirit knows that her wish to please others, comes only from the inability to accept herself, masking her person with her own showings, as she dances away from herself and everyone in her life.

The spirit within chooses to let go of her own created image. She becomes real, creating Love for herself, sharing it gently with everyone and becomes the most beautiful dancer on the grand ballroom floor of her life. The renaissance for this special woman in her total magnificence, captivates all with her dance of total Love and complete freedom.

Other men and women sit on the precipice of death, by not living, not even creating an image of an aging beauty queen or football hero of yesteryear. They choose a nerdiness so boring, that they put everyone asleep around them, including the plants and animals.

There is always hope; however, for all in our nerd

kingdoms, just as in heaven. As mother nature wakes up the world with thunder and lightning, cleansing the air, creating streams of water for everything thirsty with rain drops falling on every head, a bolt of lightning explodes the wonderful magnificence within the non-living, near death, depressed and rejected folks of the chosen land.

Pow! Power for all! The true spirits within surface with dimensions of human electricity far beyond anyone's imagination.

They soar into their magnificence as a rock star gyrates life to the adolescents of the times. The complete sexuality, seductiveness and joy radiate with all, as the unliving being mutates to beautiful, totally Loving men and women strutting their stuff as only they really can, on their new found dance floors of their lives.

Just as the platypuses in nature amble and scramble alone through the marshes and swamps of their lives, the spirits within all can share their attractions to each other, gently and softly connecting heart to heart. The platypuses leave their loneliness and find a mate, touching each other so gently with their webbed feet. Then they swim in ultimate respect and love for each other, as they share this special dance of life, when all stands still in the

Love Dances

universe and the spirits within new baby platypuses choose these special parents in their chosen marshes.

The joy of Love and the magnificence of being real, without the images and judgments of what one should and should not be, creates a special respect for oneself and inner peace that is comforting for each person in the chosen land. As one passes along its chosen life's path, moving and being with your magnificence encompasses all with an incredible dance of security, peace and harmony with unconditional Love for everyone and everything.

Dancing With Perceptions

  *T*he spirit within every person is unique and chooses its own life's path, always in concert with the essence of God. The soft inner connections of its being are shared with all in the chosen land as fine threads ever so delicate, connecting soul to soul, mind to mind, heart to heart, so on and so on.

  What is and what isn't, is seen only through the eyes or felt through the hearts of each spirit as one dances with perceptions. The verbalizations and body images sent from one person to another, may not be received as it was intended to be sent by the other. It really is only as it is perceived.

  As a small child perceives his or her parents, leaders of his or her church, the politicians of the land, and every other being in the community, it is only as it is to the inner spirit of that child. Responses, comments and reactions create dance steps in each person, sometimes to

LOVE DANCES

the same beat, sometimes with totally strange notes and steps.

Perceptions, how wonderful they can be for one and how different, even painful, for another. The inner sensitivities sometimes completely change the intent of a message, sometimes creatively, sometimes with hurt, sometimes with fear of rejection, sometimes even with the fear of Love.

Traditions from the church leaders, politicians and the elders of the families and community cast learned perceptions for each person. When someone says or does something, it is learned in the same way as the walls surrounding the person are learned and built, with their own bricks and mortar.

A smile and raised eyebrow in one land means fun and excitement, while in another family or land it means distrust, deceit or seduction of a physical opportunity. Masks of perception are worn and change with the traditions of each family, culture and religion.

The perceptions and their expectations, as learned and not learned because the soft inner spirit always knows the truth with total Love for all, dance to all in its universe. From the classical to the most modern of music of the

DANCING WITH PERCEPTIONS

times, the universal language transcends every culture and country, yet is perceived by the youth one way, the adults another and the elders may choose not to dance at all.

Visual arts, crafts and creations of people are perceived with that special dance of incredible beauty by the spirits within each person. Others may not perceive beauty or even that the creation was an art, craft or anything of value at all.

Just as in mother nature, aphids choose to suck the life from the roses and ranunculus. They dance with each other for that split second when all in the universe stands still and a spirit chooses to join its aphid family of choice. The ants join the dance, with opportunity in establishing their own farms of life through the farming of their own aphids.

One's dance steps shift in perception, just as the birds serve another by harvesting the insects from the backs of the water buffalo and the barnacles attach themselves to whales, mussels and oysters. People from one land to another serve each other in trade, sharing products and assimilating culture, language, arts, music and athletic events as the Olympics serve everyone of all ages without limits or judgments.

Love Dances

Perceptions of death as the aphid to its flower, may really be the beautiful dance of life for another. One serves another in special concert, maintaining the soft balance of nature with man, from the forests to the flowers and all the people and critters who choose to dance among the leaves and blossoms, with people from every land.

Every person and being chooses their own dance of perception, from trash to treasure. Traditions and judgments may obstruct or enhance the total freedom to extend beyond the limits of one's up-bringing, and dance in the grandest ballroom of time with unconditional Love, peace and harmony, setting the inner spirit free for eternity.

Dancing With Forgiveness

As the elders of the land cast their marks and impressions on all the chosen people, traditions are established in the same way generation upon generation. The inner spirit with the true essence of God, knows the real meaning of life and unconditional Love for one's family, friends and all in its world.

From time to time, a spirit chooses its own dance of opinions and the way it does its own thing. Sometimes, one may choose a special flower child to share its dance of Love in a new way.

The leaders of the church, politicians of the land and all of the other elders may be shocked by the new uniqueness of people choosing a different lifestyle, living as they choose. Sometimes, this lifestyle is only personal as one dances solo with one of his or her own kind, or as a couple with different values and ways.

At that time in the universe, when all stands still for

LOVE DANCES

that split second, a new spirit has the opportunity to choose a new life. A newly created child chooses its path of life and Loves, sometimes from Love, sometimes in passion and sometimes simply as a duty for one or both partners. Sharing Love and being intimate may be a totally different dance of life and a unique way to heaven.

One of the partners in a couple may enjoy one set of traditions, while another may believe differently. Sometimes one has values consistent and comfortably similar with the other partner, sometimes not.

As the communications between the two grow and change, opinions, feelings and values may be shared, or withheld, as the walls of the traditions of the chosen land are built. A person in a relationship chooses a new choice, sometimes from rebellion, sometimes out of clear motive.

This new dance is experienced only by the one changing steps on its own dance floor of life. It is unique and may not be in concert with the traditions of the land. This dance may be ever so subtle or bold and blatant, shocking all around.

Mothers and fathers of the new found being, may gasp, "Where did I go wrong?" Others may see the dance as creative, with the same flair that the mother and father has yearned for in their own identity, or lack of identity as it might be.

No matter what age, the inner spirit chooses to try its wings of a new found life. One now dances with openness and freedoms that it has always known within, yet, was holding back from the fear of disapproval or possible rejection from all around.

The elders may condescendingly wriggle a finger of disapproval at the new found dance of a teenager, experimenting with passion, style or folderol. While others, may simply ask, "What is going on?"

The dance of difference and change occurs at any age and can happen within any person. The solo partner in a relationship of service to one's church, family member or friend, may choose to leave this arena and dance with a new partner. A dance with such great inner passion, that Love is shared for the first time, in a new way.

Change and images of change reverberate throughout the chosen land, fanning the fires of gossip and the flames of judgments as one leaves the traditions of his or her teachings.

Married couples may appear to be the happiest of all

LOVE DANCES

as they create the ideal home, fill it with contented children and accomplish incredible things at their jobs of choice. They serve their church, in the true spirit of worship, as they have been taught.

The couple continues with the expectations of all, by planting the geraniums of their lives, adding a white picket fence surrounding all with safety and lots of security. The true inner spirits may feel trapped, even as though life had been snuffed out, by the traditions of their partners or elders in the land.

They choose a new dance, sometimes strutting their stuff with each other in a new way. Sometimes the inner pain of a person is so great, they choose a romantic interlude with another, bolting from all traditions and acceptable behavior in marriage and the laws of traditions in their chosen land.

The moments shared are complete bliss from the perceptions of their pain and regrets. All discomfort is set free as they frolic as they choose, leaving the realities of their daily life and risking everyone and all in this life.

If caught in their dance of infidelity, they beg forgiveness or discard their life and family. They then may choose to create a new life without dealing with the insecurities and dishonesties that created the pain and passion in the first place.

One can Love and one can cherish as the trees, flowers and birds can grow in mother nature. When trees lean on each other, all growth is stunted, just as a couple stunts each other's growth with judgments and traditions of trying to always work on and to control the other.

Every tree must be set free to stand alone, eventually and totally sharing the freedom of a strong trunk, open boughs and beautiful leaves. Each grows, straight, tall and healthy in the golden rays of the day. The inner spirit of every person knows the same need for Love and freedom from the judgments and dependencies of others, making every choice for oneself, accepting this choice with total responsibility.

When one chooses to be free, with total respect and confidence for oneself, they forgive all within and everyone in the chosen land. Complete comfort and the joy of living is again created, as it was always in the inner spirit from day one of its chosen birth.

Just as the beaver may independently harvest the river birches as it likes, it may defy the laws and traditions of the chosen beavers in its world. The rebellious beaver

Love Dances

may swim and do its thing with another, but in the end is welcomed home to its hut in the pond with the ultimate dance of acceptance and unconditional Love by the other beavers.

The highest compliment of Love is the total acceptance of another without judgment. This grandest of all dances of life is the dance of forgiveness, with total Love, caring and freedom for one's partner, mate, children, parents, grandparents, neighbors or anyone from the chosen land or any other land in the universe.

The dance of forgiveness soars with classic beauty and respect by all in the highest regard. This ultimate dance creates Love, peace and harmony to every being in its own world and frees each spirit to find its own special path to heaven.

Dancing With Trust

At the dawning of the inner spirit's chosen life, a baby enjoys its first breath with the chosen people in its life. All is trusting and all is beautiful as the child comes into its family, created with the true blessings of God.

The parents, family members, friends, community leaders and all in its world, including the gifts of mother nature, create a beautiful dance of security for the birth and early days of the blessed child. The lives and Love of all around, caress the baby with the blanket of security as it interacts in its chosen world.

Just as the golden rays of sunlight follow the darkness of night, the smile of contentment and security beams from the spirit within this baby. The journey from its place of birth may be one of smoothness with the grace of mother nature, or one of a changing environment with diamonds of rain, feathers of snow or cleansing winds

Love Dances

blowing out the old and in the new.

A chosen blending of heredity and environment for the inner spirit of this child, dances along its path of life in its chosen land. The blessed gift of one's ancestors and the possible teachings from all in its home, community and chosen land set the course for a wonderful voyage so totally unique, yet with special qualities of its chosen people.

The judgments, opinions and traditions of the elders establish the ambiance of life for this child, this teenager and finally this adult. The mirror of its life, its security or lack of security radiate from all around. The political freedoms of its people, the sensitivities within and about, the harshness or comfort of the environmental elements and all else, create the dance of trust within the chosen one.

The confidence of the parents reflect trust and confidence in the child. The guidance and wisdom of the grandparents mirror lessons of life far beyond the brief years that the child has danced in its chosen land. The teachings of the church leaders, statesmen of the government, and community elders share a vision of trust and security for the special one.

Dancing With Trust

The dance of security changes as the people and land change around it. Sometimes within the chosen person, a dance of interpretation and perception sees its chosen world only through its own eyes and in its own heart. The inner spirit grows and experiences, just as in mother nature.

With the changing of the seasons, all in the gardens recreate life with the fleeting burst of color and chivalry of the yellow daffodils in its gift of springtime. The spring turns to summer with the constancy of bluebells always there, sharing beauty and nectar for the child and bees.

The dog days of February in the southern hemisphere and its partner of August in the northern part of our own world, cast a reflection of what could have been and what is ahead in the teachings of life. The dance of harvest soars into the falls of life after the plantings of the seeds of life, cultivation of the crops and a weeding of the unwanted.

On to the winter of one's time, when a renaissance of buds are created for next year's fruit on the trees, restoration of energy in the crocus and in every bird and animal. Each being reconnects for that split second when

Love Dances

all stands still in the universe. New spirits choose life for the births of new babies in the nests of thrushes and caribou calves, dancing from the snows of their parents to new blessed lives in their springtime.

Trust is created as the world turns on its axis, creating the incredible life cycle for all. The inner spirits of every person dance in the meadows of trust and security, knowing within, that Love is unconditional, peace bonds neighbors and all from other lands, and harmony reigns on earth and in heaven.

Dancing With Winning

The chosen family does all to create the most open, successful home filled with Love, caring and the nurturing aspects that any person can give to their children and loved ones. The inner spirit of the child, choosing its family, has its life's path choreographed with special dances of lessons and wonderful experiences.

The traditions of all the families, church leaders, politicians, teachers and sport commentators establish the various dances of games. These games vary from the soccer field, to the basketball court and into the interpersonal lives of every person.

The judgments of the elders, as well as the desire to compete in games of all kinds, focus the winnings and losings for every event. No matter how they look, the games of life, baseball, cards or monopoly constitute fun with one's attitude.

The dance of the competition sets one person

LOVE DANCES

opposing another or a team working together as a tight-knit family preparing for its field game against another team. One wins, one loses as the game is played, determined by the traditions of the chosen land.

From person to person and land to land in the world, the rules may vary as do the ingredients of the sport, the money in the monopoly game or the faces of the royalty on the playing cards. The inner spirits of all competing in the games of choice, know that the purpose of having fun within and sharing with everyone else is what it's all about.

The Olympic gold medal winner of a wonderful ice skating performance exudes the dance of joy for that person, her or his country and all to enjoy the grace, beauty and desire to share one's talent, discipline and accomplishments. It's not about beating the other entrants, but the inner beauty and talent within a person, shining with unconditional Love and accomplishment with all in one's world.

Relationships are like the games of time. The dance of winning may not appear as we think it should look, as taught by the traditions all around us.

Families have their values, as do all in the chosen

Dancing With Winning

land. Loud voices of rights and wrongs are shouted about in the community, its schools and on the televisions in the homes of the chosen land.

People, throughout time, reflect the judgments of rights and wrongs, conquering one nation to control others to make themselves seem more powerful, more knowing and to reap the spoils from others. The wars of people, as in nature, do not make peace and harmony as one nation steals the human and environmental rights from others.

Similar battles of beings are waged in mother nature with the bull elk or stallion trying to conquer more than their share of cow elks or mares. The battles rage, often resulting in loss for all as the horns of the bull elk are locked, can not be separated resulting in death to both and not protection to the cows. The stallions injure each other, in fatally breaking a leg, or fighting while predators capture their herds.

As in mother nature, the spirits within know and accept unconditionally, each person and thing dancing with winning for all in its world. With wisdom for all to win, the spirit of the soft inner voice speaks and shares, in the true essence of God, Love and respect for each other.

LOVE DANCES

Winning for all on the football field, may mean the inner joy of playing the game and being proud of making it to their super bowl game in their world, no matter if it is the eight man championship. The same win, win attitude occurs in a marriage, when both partners give and share unconditional Love, removing all walls and barriers. The inner spirits connect in their universe, all stands still and a new spirit has an opportunity to choose this special couple for his or her family.

The dance of winning creates peace and harmony with true unconditional Love for all in the chosen land, as well as all the people in other lands. All beings enjoy the opportunity of playing this game, living life with total Love and setting each spirit free to be its all, with God, in its universe.

Dancing With Excellence

*W*ith passing years, the chosen child matures along its beautiful path of life. Ongoing interactions occur with parents, family members, the congregation of its church of choice, and the politicians with their rhetoric of what is, what should be and what the opponent is not doing.

Beliefs, values, cultural acceptabilities are imprinted carefully, yet sometimes in total opposition to or rebellion from the soft inner spirit of the chosen person.

The rights and wrongs of the people establish the things in life one is supposed to strive for, creating the goals and objectives for all. Before a dance of excellence begins, it seems that the people in the chosen land get hung up on continually working on another person, in lieu of themselves.

This energy becomes a dance of wanting to change a loved one, one's partner, whether a mirror of one's own

Love Dances

kind or not, or a spouse. It transcends upon all in the chosen land; the judgments, values, traditions and all the things that will, supposedly, bring happiness to everyone.

Sometimes it might look like marrying the proper young lady or gentleman because they come from a "proper" or "good" family. Sometimes a choice of career is the ideal, whether a doctor, lawyer, beggar or thief, depending on the mores and traditions of given people in a chosen land.

The rights and wrongs within one, or the society of choice, culminate to a level of perfectionism. All energy is focused on the opinions of that person striving for this ultimate perfect life, its perfect values, perfect rigid walls to keep everyone away by walling one in, and perfect things for everyone.

Perfectionism and rigidity chase away the ultimate power, flexibility and excellence in a person. Flexibility represents the dance of complete openness, acceptance of another's values, unconditionally.

The total person, in concert with the soft inner spirit, enjoys dancing with excellence. This special dance is a journey through life with wonderful friends, animals and plants.

Dancing With Excellence

Flexibility soars in the dance of excellence. The inner spirit, with true unconditional Love for oneself, in the true essence of God, shares complete acceptance, without judgment, its Love and caring for all around.

The abundance is the same, as in mother nature, when all of the elements, wind, rain and mother earth, serve all on this planet. It nurtures life, sharing the earth's wealth of animals, plants, jewels and life itself.

Each inner spirit knows to protect mother earth and all of the plants and animals to maintain the soft balance where all live in harmony. People, with their lust for perfection to do their thing, rigidly exploit others and their own country or the lands of other people or things.

Caution is shared for all people to be flexible in their choices and to protect the environment. Provide the continuous opportunity for life on earth as it is in heaven, for eternity.

The dance of excellence in the land of the equator, may be the abundant dance of the hippopotamus. Mother nature blends the balance of nature in the open spaces of their homeland in Africa. This special home has the watering holes to sustain the plants for its meals and a safe nursery for the chosen spirits of the baby hippos,

LOVE DANCES

after that split second in the universe, when all stood still and the parent hippopotamuses chose to share their special Love with each other.

Perfectionism, greed and searching for the rights for a single man or woman, can exploit this fine balance of life in the African watering hole. The flexible respect of life for all beings and things create an excellent dance for the critters, persons and plants. This dance maintains the soft balance of the wonderful journey through life, for generation after generation in our chosen world.

No one person, animal or plant ever achieves the realm of total perfection. Someone or something always tips over the basket of security, when one believes that he or she is perfect and knows all of the rights and wrongs.

Perfection is brought about by fear of others' judgments or rejections. Perfection is also the wall of doing something incorrectly in one's own eyes or breaking any or all of the traditional rights or wrongs of the land.

Perfectionism takes away strength and energy, just as the dance of excellence creates security, family closeness and the strength of complete teamwork at work, on the playing field, in one's community, church or chosen land. Excellence is found within the spirit of everyone, when

Dancing With Excellence

pride, joy and satisfaction are created.

The special beauty and complete freedom from all restrictions are created and enjoyed in the dance of excellence. It dances through relationships, when unconditional Love is shared for oneself, one's mate, family, church members, friends and with all in the chosen land.

Just as in heaven, one experiences complete acceptance, inner peace and harmony in dancing with excellence.

Dancing With Success

Generation upon generation establish the traditions and values in the chosen land. As each new spirit chooses life with its own family and community friends, it joins a selected space of established mores, cultures and expectations.

The inner spirit of this blessed child, in the true essence of God, and all from heaven, experiences unconditional Love and truth at the beginning of its birth. This inner knowing of trust and freedom follows and guides the chosen person throughout its special life.

With the growth and maturing of the child to adolescence and on to adulthood, rewards, praises and recognition follow each action it chooses or is asked to do. Whether it is picking up a teddy bear, Lego blocks or planting a petunia in the garden, the blessed one is acknowledged for varying and ever-changing tasks.

Kind words for a-not-so-kind aunt or uncle, still reap

Dancing With Success

a verbal accolade for acknowledgement of the words, whether true from the heart or not. Conflict and castigations occur when young people or adults alike, break the rules of the traditions and laws of the chosen land.

Rebellion, creativity and new lifestyles modify the stale traditions and expectations of yesteryear. The elder family members, church leaders and politicians of the land are shocked by what is happening to the youth and young adults of today. A generation passes and what was not tradition is now tradition. How delightful the dance of change can be.

The dance steps of success are measured, but are ever-changing by the traditions of the given cultures, values and expectations of people from every land. The religions, political climates and essence of each nation present the customs, and what is hot and what is not, for the aspiring folks, from young to old.

Success is failure for some, while failure is success for others. The inner spiritual, silver thread connecting each other, is soft, gentle and true. It knows the respect of giving 100%, in achieving what one desires in life.

This creation of dancing with success, may be finding

Love Dances

that special person with whom your heart and soul connect, with energy transporting you from your life to share with theirs. The dancing partners soar in the rainbows of life, when all in the universe stands still and a new spirit may choose this special family, basking in the success of true and total Love for oneself and each other.

Mother nature joins the orchestration of life, dancing as moonbeams dance their halos across the knolls and meadows when all nocturnal creatures and plants connect in their own excellence of life and Love. The bats from the belfry and the cats from their lairs, lazar a connection through their radars of Love or their midnight melodies that awaken all to the symphony of their mating calls.

How big or small doesn't matter in Love and lust, only the true unconditional Love that one lioness shares with her king of the jungle, no matter what this jungle may look like. The dance of success is within one, creating complete satisfaction within, then sharing it and serving all around in one's world.

The dance with success, never comes or is created from others, the laws of the land, or the leaders of the church. It bubbles up from the soul of our being, just as in heaven, with total freedom, acceptance and pride for the ability to share with others and the beauty of the lands and castles where we dance.

God is within us, as we choreograph our dances of life. Its successes and our special soul mate share Love and give the birth of life to other spirits awaiting the beautiful journey. The peace and harmony of knowing true respect and passion for ourselves and others, cast an aura of beauty and freedom for every being in the chosen land.

Dancing With Sexuality

*W*hen a male and female unite totally in that split second when all in the universe stands still, a new spirit may choose this couple as their parents for their future life in their chosen land. The dance of being begins, in concert with the dance with sexuality.

The chosen parents bring special, unique dance steps into the blessed child's life, in the true essence of God. The traditions, roles of each parent and the identity of the child and young adult are formed, by relating to its chosen parents and all in the chosen land.

From the days of other millenniums, hunters and gatherers spent most of their lives in search for and sharing food with a small group of humans. Courses of people and rivers, as well as climate, changed and brought together the early communities on the fertile banks of the Euphrates, Tigris, Colorado and Nile waters.

With the sharing of community life, came new dances

for all to do. Certain duties and responsibilities were created, then became expected for the men and women of all ages, as well as the children.

As civilizations grew and changed, the members of this chosen land cultivated crops, founded irrigation systems, continued the quest of hunting or tamed beasts for milk and meat, housed birds for eggs and meat and established commerce by trading with exchanges. People in these new communities formed new traditions and new customs.

The spirits never age in time, just choose new life paths, learning the new dances of survival, with customs, giving one land and its people a different look from another civilization. Boys will be boys as are men, men, and women will be women, but with the pomp and pageantry, as mirrored by the customs of a given people in a chosen time, in the chosen land.

One generation follows its ancestors. The dance of life changes its beat with each cycle of life, moving the gifts of wisdom to the next generation as a grandparent embraces the grandchild, with unconditional Love, sharing of the customs of old and what is new, as they see it.

Love Dances

Each spirit from birth until death, chooses all along its path, its own dances, including the images, behaviors and sexual preference for its life. Part is heredity as is intelligence, sensitivity and every physical drive; part is the environment, with all of the customs, religious and political values.

The wonderful blend of all cast the maleness and femaleness for each being, as Macbeth and his Lady danced with their sexuality in the castles of time. Each being experiences a blend of males and females from day one, suckling from the breast of life, sharing Love, passion and strength of purpose.

As parents, grandparents and every person interact with the children, one's identity comes into its own shining starlight. When parents experience difficulties with their own identity and feelings about the opposite sex, the child and young adult mirror the same insecurities, resentments, and lack of trust in themselves.

After playing with playmates of one's own sex, with dolls and sporting balls, puberty explodes into one's new dance of life. They leave their own same sex friends to dance a new dance, alone, attracting the opposite sex for attention and folderol, whatever that might look like.

Dancing With Sexuality

The dance of life is one that is ever-changing, when one is more comfortable with her own girlfriend or his own boyfriend of yesterday, when the pressures of society were absent. Everyone accepted all children unconditionally with total Love and understanding.

Societal pressures of dating, marriage and sexual identities create unrealistic images of being too sexy for oneself, as the ultimate girl or guy, often crumbling the inner security and walling off the real, true unconditional Loving. There are pure spirits behind the lip gloss, swim suits and sensuous dances of females or the macho, manic roles of the males.

It is no wonder the fragile spirit of youth and young adults vacillate with the pain and glory of the relationships of their parents, the expectations of society, and their own inner passions for sharing Love, value and physicalness with their chosen partner. The soul mate connects with his or her true soul mate for the first time, lasting throughout all time, in the chosen land and in heaven.

Most choose the openness of a wonderful mate to share Love, emotions, and dreams creating their special memories. All stands still for a split second on their

Love Dances

blessed wedding night, and a new spirit chooses its life with these special parents in the chosen land.

Others dance in the mirrors of service, sometimes with total commitment to God and their church, their family or a friend. Everything is beautiful, no matter what it looks like to others or to the people of other lands and beliefs. Love is within the soul. The more it is shared in a caring and Loving way, the more the spirit is set free and fulfilled.

Just as in mother nature, the robin dances the first dance of Spring, when the azure eggs are laid in the tresses of the tree tops. The new spirits of life choose their robin family after that split second when all stood still in the universe, as the true Love was shared between the robin parents.

The dew of evening sends life to the trees and plants, as each flower blooms and shares its maleness and femaleness. The pollens of their lives, fertilize each other and create the beautiful life cycle for all new plants and trees.

The dance with sexuality is ever-changing and acceptable with the same passion and respect that each generation shares with its next generation. New tunes of

Dancing With Sexuality

life, wild and crazy dances gyrate within and across people in the chosen land.

All stands still for a split second in true unconditional Love, when one proudly shares her femaleness with herself then with his maleness and he shares his maleness with himself and then with her femaleness. Dancing with sexuality creates life, peace and harmony for all in the chosen land and throughout the world.

Dancing With Sexual Intimacy

Relationships of the chosen people in the chosen land are as ever-changing as the winds of mother nature. From the beaming smile of a newly found acquaintance to the deep connection of family and friends, the inner spirits of all seek a special relationship filled with unconditional Love, passion and a zest for life.

The special closeness of sharing friendship, fun activities, creating laughter and joy, and a commitment to be there for another, brings girls together with girls, boys with boys, women with men and men with women. There are unlimited relationships founded on that special respect and trust for another, heart to heart, soul to soul, regardless of one's maleness or femaleness.

As we seek relationships of unconditional Love in a most unique way, we bring together all our values, beliefs, sexuality and traditions from others that we have chosen as our own. The dance steps of life change as one perceives oneself or another in a different light.

The girl next door grew up with wonderful freckles, pig tails and climbed the neighborhood trees. Then something happened only as the inner spirit has chosen, in the true essence of God, she is transformed into the most beautiful woman in the world.

The same process soars in the handsome, sensitive man, from the scrawny kid with funny, gawky looks and clumsiness of not knowing. Sometimes opposites attract, sometimes images of being the same as the hearts within open up and share their true person.

This true, whole person radiates his maleness or her femaleness with gentle, unconditional Love, inner beauty and sincerity without pretensions of what a male or female is to be, in order to be sexy and accepted as the super hero or heroine. The identity of one is muddied when one tries to emulate a famous movie star, rock super star, or leading politician in the land.

The dating game is a game of enchantment, captivating each other in a special connection when hearts meet, the souls within one's eyes beam true acceptance, Love and honesty. The sharing of these memories carry us through a relationship to another level, so beautiful,

LOVE DANCES

vulnerable and committed to risking all.

The fires of passion rage within as the desires of sharing the ultimate Love and physicalness grow to a size beyond comprehension. The burning, tingling sensations electrify all as two inner spirits connect as soul mates, and exude Love for all around to experience.

The sharing of this Love, in the magnificent concert of life and the creation of new life, flies as free as the wind. Values and minds dance in a syncopated rhythm, emotions relate, traditions blend acceptance with all other traditions and the ultimate occurs.

Everything in the universe stands still, as the couple commits complete unconditional Love for each other and dances with sexual intimacy. They soar together as one body in complete harmony and passion for life to be created as a new spirit, or spirits as the time might be, chooses this couple for life, with the total Love of God.

The dance of sexual intimacy is not about pleasurable techniques or being the ultimate lover. Devices, pre-intimacy activities or post play are only traditions, some old, some new. True Love sharing is not about watching one perform from one's head or almost being totally separate from one's body or body parts.

Dancing With Sexual Intimacy

When total Love is shared between two beautiful beings, the dance of sexual intimacy encompasses all. The dance steps, in unison, flow without limits, heart to heart, spirit to spirit, sensitivity to sensitivity, physicalness to physicalness and on and on. Sexual intimacy is part of this beautiful sharing of unconditional Love, passion, respect and freedom with each other.

Mother nature salutes and embraces every bird, bear, tree, mountain and stream in Love. The herons of the chosen land dance in unison, creating regally the ultimate sharing of Love, when all stands still for that split second and the spirit chooses to join the heron family in the secluded willowed island in the stream of its chosen life.

The snows of either earth's pole cast the violins of life, when the polar bears growl a chorus of Love before, then during and after the ultimate intimate connection, when all stands still in its icy world, and a new spirit or spirits choose to be twin polar bear cubs in the springtime of their lives.

The rain forest caresses the air with aromas, droplets of life for all and green, giving beauty and life, when the pollens and seeds of the mahogany trees share the ultimate, when all stands still in their life, and new

LOVE DANCES

mahogany trees emerge to replenish the harvested trees of yesterday. Life continues as intimacy is shared between trees, furnishing a home of Love for all critters, birds and people choosing Love and life in the special world of the chosen rain forest.

The mountains, with all of their gold and diamonds, share the Love of strength and majesty to kiss the clouds creating snows for tomorrow's water and protection to all in the small Swiss valley. This valley is beautiful with the summer breezes waving flowers sharing their pollens and birds, bees and cows enraptured in life with Love itself.

Each droplet of water casts its prism of life, joining with another and another, until a stream is born. This wonderful habitat creates life for all from the crevasses of a mountain top to the fertile plains feeding all with grain, animals and other plants.

The abundance is for all in this chosen land to dance with food so tasteful, healthy and life providing. This exemplifies a balance in mother nature without the need for pesticides to kill another.

Unconditional Love abounds and culminates as part of the ultimate sharing in sexual intimacy, no matter what it looks like. The true inner spirits connect softly and gently in the streams of life as fine white threads, with every person, plant, animal and bird.

The dance with sexual intimacy soars freely with all in the chosen land. Love dances today, tomorrow and forever as in the kingdom of heaven.

Dancing With Birth

The soft inner spirit within every being possesses a special freedom, Love and courage for its chosen path of life in the chosen land. Its dance at birth is totally unique and is a wonderful blend of heredity, cultures and traditions as one joins its chosen people.

The celebration of the dance at birth is the greatest gift of all, in the full essence of God. The unconditional Love, protection, maternal and paternal instincts of parenting at birth are the ultimate in caring.

The miracle of creating life recreates continuing Love, the future of a family and a level of inner beauty and peace far beyond one's expectations. All in the chosen family join in the experience of birth when a new spirit chooses life, no matter which wonderful family is blessed by life's gift in the universe.

Elders in families, churches and communities enjoy the celebrations of pending births of its members.

Dancing With Birth

Dancing with birth occurs far in advance of the event itself.

The dance of adolescence and youth gyrates the dating games when boy meets girl and girl meets boy. Young men and women choose, or choose not to choose, various dances of courtship as they search for that special connection when heart meets heart.

Spirits unite in a powerful connection called Love. Sometimes the elders refer to this Love as "true Love", puppy Love, infatuation or simply hormones, that are too hot to handle.

Cold showers may rain on a parade of passion. Disparaging remarks only whet the youths' Love dance, no matter what it looks like in the chosen land. Bliss energizes the connection when a man and a woman unite in a relationship, no matter the age or at what level of unitedness.

They soar together in the incredible dance of Love, sharing, teasing, nipping and nibbling the coos of commitment and their meaning of future lives together. The couple dances closer to each other in every way, living in the here and now, planning future lives together and telling funny stories about family members.

Love Dances

Sometimes the connection is a game of image and what should be, or rebellion from what should be. Sometimes the relationship is a true connection of the inner souls finding each other in their universe for another dance of time.

The commitment to each other is shared in a celebration of Love, in marriage, living together, or coming and going to and from the rain forest as is the custom in their chosen land. The celebration of unconditional Love soars to new heights when all in the universe stands still, and their Love is consummated in the beauty of sexual intimacy as part of their ultimate Love for each other.

The fine red thread connects the inner spirits of each other; creating Love, dancing heart to heart for their lives and through eternity. The supreme gift, each may choose to share with the other, in the true essence of God, is the gift of new life when each shares soft, true, unconditional Love for the other. Then the ultimate occurs, when a new spirit chooses to join this couple as its chosen family.

The symphonies of other spirits within every bird, bear and tree play dances so beautiful, so meaningful, that mother nature embraces with Love all in her world.

Dancing With Birth

Members of every species pair, even if for only the briefest of brief moments. Life is created as all beings, stand still in the universe sharing their Love totally, opening the doors of life for any spirit to join its family of its chosen kind in its chosen world.

Love conquers all. A giraffe chooses its special mate, embracing and standing still for that split second, and a new giraffe joins its giraffe family in the Africa of its life.

Finches of every shape and color, sing a courtship song of intrigue, passion, then commitment, when all stands still in their lives and a new union creates a spirit within tomorrow's egg in its intricately sculpture nest. This same nest houses its birth a few days later, as the spirit of this finch chooses its family in the bush of Australia.

Dancing with birth is the dance of life, its passion and the continuance of chosen beings throughout the universe. Dancing with birth creates the ultimate celebration of unconditional Love, peace and harmony of each couple, its offspring and all in its chosen land.

Dancing With Service

The soft inner spirit dancing along life's path is ever-changing and creates wonderful lessons for it to live. The freedom of giving to another propels the spirit to a new level of inner strength, security and meaning to the chosen person.

The dance of giving to others serves the chosen person, in the true essence of God, growing each day in every way. The dance of service is deep, caring and fulfilling with the opportunity to caress the tired shoulders of a loved one, to place a bandage on the scraped knee of the roller blading youth or to provide Love to one out of discord with oneself or the entire chosen world that day.

The teachings of the elders in all their wisdom and steeped cultural values exemplify the traditions for all in the chosen community. The elder family members, the church leaders, school teachers and politicians in the chosen land blend the traditions of what to do for whom

DANCING WITH SERVICE

and when to do it.

Manners, etiquette and respect for one another weave together the traditions, values and social mores for all in the chosen land. What is acceptable during one generation, becomes passe with the advancement of another generation.

While some social courtesies remain constant in the dance of respect and regard for another, other protocols of society may change, end or remain the same. Some members of society spend countless hours judging the acceptable behaviors of all in the chosen land, gossiping at the shocking defiance of some in forgetting the traditions in respecting one another.

No matter how the social wrapping appears on the chosen people dancing through their lives, the inner spirit knows the true expression of sharing and caring in service to another. Other spirits within certain persons have this lesson to learn during their chosen lifetimes.

True respect for another begins within each spirit and its knowing of Love, caring and service for each other. Radiance shines as the dance of service, even in the supermarket, when a strong youth or hassled mother assists an elderly shopper with her bag of sugar.

Love Dances

Dancing with service occurs with all beings in every land throughout the world. The dance is different for every person. It may be seen at a country club party, when a member shares a beverage and dance with another, creating beautiful memories for each other. The steps are the same, yet different, for the farmer in the country sharing a hot cup of coffee and a piece of banana cream pie for a drop-in friend or shirt-tailed relative on a cold blustery day.

The spider monkeys of the jungle join in the dance of service with each other. They serve themselves and each other in grooming the soft skins, sensitively, sharing Love and being caring.

Mother nature encompasses all in service to each other. The trees, the birds and animals bond together forming the forests of the pines, the wind breaks of the Lombardy poplars and swallows announcing the first days of summer.

All stands still in the universe, when two share the ultimate service to each other, with total Love, and a new spirit may choose to join the family of its kind for its incredible life in the chosen place of its world. The family of plants, birds, animals and people dance in service to

Dancing With Service

each other. They create life, Love, peace and harmony throughout their chosen land.

The more the inner spirits serve one another and everything in the ecology of the chosen land, the greater the satisfaction of that truly joyful feeling. Dancing with service through giving is the ultimate gift of unconditional Love, in the true essence of God. The vision of life grows within each chosen person in service, as the spiritual energy reigns supreme in the chosen land.

Dancing With Your Body

*A*t that split second in the universe when all stands still, a couple sharing their ultimate Love with each other offers the opportunity for a spirit to choose life, its family as well as all of its ancestors. The dance of freedom begins with the wonderful physical, mental, emotional and spiritual traits for this chosen life, with its own family.

The genetic traits that are chosen include all of the humanly possible attributes of this blessed child, in the true essence of God, the creator. The dance of life begins with its cherished body, so chosen, at that split second when new life was created.

The body serves as a temple for the soft inner spirit with all of its knowingness and energy to soar through its special chosen life. Dancing with your body begins at birth and continues throughout this person's entire life and until the beautiful transformation to heaven occurs.

Dancing With Your Body

What you get is what you get. Some perceive their body as a blessing, while others view it with certain limitations. It is only perception. This perception is often directly connected to the well-beingness, Love and security of the chosen family and the chosen land.

The spiritual shift of comfort with one's chosen body is ever-changing and always growing, no matter what this growth may look like. From the feeling of a victim of genes not as equal as those of another, to realizing the beautiful possibilities for all, one feels fortunate with what they have. This good feeling includes confidence, about what their inner spirit has chosen and what lessons it is going to share in this lifetime.

Making one's brown eyes blue, or the green of the sea, shifts as technology and arts of medicines shift. We add straighteners to curly hair and curls to straight hair, as well as lighteners or darkeners to the same or different hair.

What makes one feel good about oneself is not in the searching, but finding the unconditional Love for oneself, not what society views as sexy, manly or acceptable. Groom as one wishes but remember only three things that you are blessed with: physical heredity, spiritual being as

LOVE DANCES

energy and your chosen land and its environment.

The metabolism, body shape, energy to exercise or to only enjoy the potatoes on the couches of life are your spiritual choices. Soar or slump as you might, God shares the beautiful gift of your chosen body. Take care of it as you choose.

The process of building walls with our bodies create wild dance steps. Some exercise to feel good, some exercise to keep people away with their muscles of masculinity and femininity, what ever that looks like. Some spend thousands of hours running, some for health and a beautiful attitude smelling the soft fragrances of the spring apricot and plum blossoms.

Others choose to run the same course, only running from oneself, their mate and their chosen family. The spiritual choice of Love for oneself, openness with others and the gifts of freedom for all are beautifully connected as a silver-blue thread to every heart and soul.

The courage of life is all encompassing in the hearts of every being including the beauties and the beasts of mother nature. No matter how frightening a Gorilla of Borneo may be, the soft gentleness, shyly shared with its family, is the same spiritual gift of life with its chosen

DANCING WITH YOUR BODY

body. The mice of the world play, scrap and get fat or thin as the abundance of their chosen environment shifts from the riches of the grain fields or the sparseness of the church's kitchen.

Dancing with your body opens up life, Love and joy as you choose. Exercise for one is the zest of walking through a shopping mall, while another is dancing with the latest beat of the musical tapes, discs and bands. Another shares beautiful memories and exciting plans strolling with a Loved one or special friend through their neighborhoods, woods or meadows of their chosen life.

The dance changes as your body changes from the first steps of a new baby, to the dance of grandparents celebrating 50 years of Love, marriage, life and their wonderful family.

Embrace your body with Love, nutrition, rest and lifestyle that creates peace and harmony for oneself. Then share this dancing with your body as a gift of health and inner beauty with every person in the chosen land.

Dancing With Food

*T*he ultimate celebration for the people in the chosen land is the celebration of abundance. The toils and troubles of sowing seeds, removing weeds, adding water, other nutrients and finally harvesting the crops of one's life, create this abundance.

Whether the literal is referenced in grains, vegetables, herbs and all that might come from mother earth, or the effort is committed to the feedings, watering and the care that serve the animals of the chosen land. The poultry, cows, goats and fishes go excellently with the grains and vegetables in creating the beautiful, bountiful dances of food.

The inner spirit of the child of God, with the chosen family in its chosen land, knows the Love, effort and all that goes into creating life and sustaining sustenance for one's body. Millenniums ago, our forefathers were hunters of beasts and gatherers of plants and berries.

Dancing With Food

Today, the people in the chosen land have changed their steps of dancing with food to hunting and gathering foods at the local supermarkets, open markets and fisheries. The chosen people search out, just as their ancestors did, that special bird, piece of beast, fish or vegetable for their family dinner.

Any family member can go to one's food market of life from the open, noisy Istanbul markets to his or her supermarket in Amsterdam with all of its finest imports. One may grow and sell their food stuffs for other food, shelter and clothing for their families and homes.

Dancing with food consumes every person in every land at some point in each day. One pays, another plays in the dance with the cabbages, spinach, carrots and artichokes in celebrating the bounty of the land, with their special families and Loved ones.

Memories, oh, those special memories, of sharing the dance of food with a Loved one, just as the times when all stands still in their universe and a new spirit has the choice to create a new life. From the first suckle of a new born baby to the piece of blackberry pie with a scoop of home made ice cream at a grandparent's home, dancing with food is a dance of Love and sharing with each other.

LOVE DANCES

As one plants his or her seeds of life, then cares for these seeds, watches them grow and then harvests tomatoes, potatoes, a cod fish or broiler chicken, the dance of food is created for one and all in the family. The preparation of food is an art, from the simplest recipes with a little salt and a sprinkle of pepper to the exotic herbs and spices, in sauces blended as lives caress the food for that special day.

The sharing of food is a time for sharing Love and thoughts with one's chosen dining partners. Communication blooms at the tables of life and is shared as the bounties of the land and seas are shared.

Sometimes, this beautiful, full table dances with a special ambiance and unique recipes with incredible food and service, in a home away from home, in the restaurants or cafes of the chosen land. The art of food selection, preparation and service reign supreme with succulent Italian pastas, Finnish fish dishes, Chinese vegetables, Mexican enchiladas, French sauces, Argentinean beef, Hungarian breads and on and on throughout every land. Special foods, differing as people and cultures differ, are prepared and shared each day with all the chosen people in the world.

Dancing With Food

Wonderful conversations occur every day as one shares with another about the happenings in the world of food, what restaurant is hot, where to find the freshest fish, which fruits of the trees are a bumper crop, both sweet and nourishing and on and on. From the haggling over a fish in the market to the candlelight of a romantic dinner in the finest restaurant of one's choice, dancing with food is a dance for everyone.

Just as the mother hen, calls her chicks when she finds tasty tidbits of sorghum and wheat grains, the spirits within every person in the chosen land call each other with their tasty findings, sometimes with an atmosphere in their home sometimes at a restaurant of choice.

Dancing with food is a dance with life and every person in our lives. Pressures and anxieties can cause one to stuff food as they stuff unsaid feelings, no matter how sensitive, no matter how lonely. Others choose to not give and receive Love as they eat so little that life may not be sustained.

The walls of protection, rejection and lack of sharing create the dance with food to wobble, shake and elude the true inner spirit of this chosen person. Loneliness and depression may trigger the nearly hidden spirit in the

LOVE DANCES

chosen person seeking warmth, satisfaction and happiness in eating and eating, or not eating at all.

When the spirit begins to open the walls, the beautiful dance flows freely throughout all parts of a person's life. Love, joy and comfort with oneself, drops grams or pounds or adds them, as the person may desire to the tummies, thighs and chins of their chosen bodies.

This unconditional Love for oneself and everyone in their chosen family and land replaces the fat or thinness with an inner radiance of honesty, caring, peace and harmony for this special person. Dancing with food touches all in their chosen lives in concert with the same Love and freedom that is shared in heaven.

Dancing With Alcohol

A toast to a new life, a toast to a new daughter-in-law, a toast to health and a toast to happiness are all traditions of people from certain chosen lands. The toasting of a glass or goblet filled with a special beverage, usually with alcohol, sets free the celebrations of the chosen people.

Many years ago, centuries for that matter, fruit juices were stored out of doors and yeasts in the air fell and fermented these beverages, adding alcohol through a chemical process. Upon drinking the beverage, persons found that a euphoric, relaxing, well-being feeling occurred.

The lessening of inhibitions flowed to all activities of their lives as the dance with alcohol was enjoyed by many. The spirits within responded in new and often different ways with the lessening of the walls surrounding the inner spirit from the chemical spirits of the alcoholic

Love Dances

beverages.

The grapes of time were cultivated with the beautiful assistance of mother nature and the juices of these fruits became wines. While grains, some malted at a later time, added to water became ales and beers.

Other fruits and vegetables when fermented in chosen lands formed different spirits with varying strengths of alcohol. These became liquors and liqueurs as named by the different societies creating their own alcoholic beverages.

As one experiments with the drinking of alcohol, traditions and expectations form, some out of complete character, as a youth or adult dances steps that are funny, obnoxious, seductive or melancholy. The unpredictabilities of imbibing form social and cultural traditions among the chosen people in different lands.

Some drinking of the spirits is fun, a little more drinking creates more of the same, then a reversal of the first and second when judgement departs, as does coordination as one stumbles into things, slurs sounds and words and on and on. Accidents follow euphoria, as does passion follow reservedness.

Dancing with alcohol affects all in the chosen lands

DANCING WITH ALCOHOL

throughout the world, as it has for millenniums. Traditions of caution are espoused by the leaders of the churches, some sacramoniously, others as a salute to the blood of men and women. Politicians sometimes toast, while others scorn the use of any spirit to which the alcohol is referred. Families enjoy and mourn the happenings associated with the alcoholic drinks.

The making of the wines, ales and spirits have become a fine art. Grapes grown in certain climates, barleys harvested from fertile soils and juniper berries picked at a certain time possess a unique flavor, change as the art of alcohol processing changes. All become the art and science of creating the best of the times for the connoisseur of the different alcohols.

The soft inner spirit within a new born child chooses its life's path with a certain family, as well as beautiful chosen people with all of their traditions, celebrations and daily happenings. Dancing with alcohol may be part of this culture as the child matures, growing to adulthood, parenthood and aging elder in the chosen land.

No matter what it looks like, the drinking of alcohol may be comfortable and in control and without the need to celebrate beyond the realm of what might be viewed as

LOVE DANCES

saneness. Enjoying wine with your bread and cheese looks one way. Having a few ales or beers after a sporting game looks another way in rollicking with fun and folderol.

It creates a different picture of life when one chooses to drink alone, lamenting what was or could have been. Each scenario differs as the chosen people choose it to be different.

Alcohol usage is a fine balance just as the thread is fine of each spirit connecting with every other spirit in the dances of life. Reflections of casual drinking with joy dance in celebration of a wedding. Other dances with alcohol share wonderful conversations with Loved ones and friends during an evening's pause to refresh or at a cocktail party.

The zealous drinking and shouting at the year's biggest game or gala affair create the illusion of too much celebration. Adding a glass of wine to that gourmet meal with a Lover makes memories in a fine dining restaurant.

One may celebrate in his or her own dance with alcohol, while another may escape from his or her reality as it is perceived. Alcohol serves one with joy, while another is served with his or her own sorrow.

DANCING WITH ALCOHOL

Some start to drink alcohol and find that they may choose not to stop as they abuse the dance of alcohol. The alcohol accentuates the walls around the inner spirit with its unconditional Love and caring, remaining buried.

Dancing with Alcohol enhances the bliss of life, its Loves, families and friends as masks change as the inhibitions lower the walls to let out joy, freedom and communications of feelings and beliefs. Perceptions and realities change as the dance steps with alcohol reverberate to the beats of different occasions.

Enjoying mother nature with a bottle of a favorite Chardonnay or Merlot and a picnic lunch creates special memories for two adults getting to know each other in their magnificence among the trees, flowers and streams of life. As the blue birds and orioles salute the couple, the blue jays want to enjoy the lunch with a camp robbing squawk.

The celebration of sharing all with each other creates romance, beyond the anticipated connection of two people, when the spirits connect heart to heart and commit Love to each other. Plans for eternity soar as the marriage in the chosen land brings all the families and friends together for the ceremony.

Love Dances

A toast is raised as stems of goblets bless the wedded couple and all dance with alcohol if so chosen. The two spirits stand still in this special Love in the universe creating the time for a new spirit or two to join this couple in the creation of life, Love and a new journey.

Enjoying the dance with alcohol for those special times creates memories of the occasion. This may mean sharing lunch and alcohol with Loved ones and special friends or as a salute to one's health, fortunes and peace on earth as it is in heaven.

The harmony of choices with the dance of alcohol is as blessed as each chosen person chooses it to be. Dancing with alcohol varies as all of the people in the chosen land vary.

Some people choose with and some without alcohol for the spirits within to partake. Let one's own judgement, inner peace, freedom of choice, true being and harmony reign with unconditional Love for oneself and each other if they choose dancing with alcohol.

Dancing With Drugs & Smoke

A soft curl of smoke spirals upward toward heaven. A puff of smoke announces a celebration of life, a traditional feast or the dangers of approaching strangers.

The aroma of a pipe's smoke permeates through a study welcoming all to join into conversations with family members and friends of all ages. The smoke filled room at a coffee break casts the challenges of a day in the work world.

The new born child has chosen its parents, family and the people of its land. The spirit within, in the true essence of God is without judgments, traditions or set opportunities for its life's path.

The cultures, traditions and all that goes on in a chosen land differ as the values, mores and tongues differ from people to people. The soft curl of smoke may be the warmth of a fireplace or cook stove welcoming all to

LOVE DANCES

the home of people, caring and sharing food, fun and festivities with Loved ones.

Groups of people dance with smoke in many unique ways, sometimes signaling a unique message, other times a simple hello from one tribe to another. While some dance to vibrations of drums and song, others dance with fire and smoke sending their own special message.

A camp fire, ritual fire or religious celebration with fire of harm and happiness tell unique stories for the chosen people, as it has been shared for generations. The smokes of the peace pipes, hand carved pipes and corn cob pipes each portray a welcoming message connecting one soul to another.

The intrigue of smoke and its meanings change with the dance steps of the times. The dance of pressure, judgments and the should-smoke-to-be-cool or should-not-to-be-healthy, vibrate throughout the traditions of the land.

One person's smoking may be a statement for acceptance, another's smoking may be an addiction for their own created stresses and strains of the walls around the soft inner spirit of the child within. Still others smoke, in whatever way they may choose, to be whom

DANCING WITH DRUGS & SMOKE

they want to be.

The spirals of smoke from the filtered cigarettes, Cuban cigars or pipes of one's choosing, blend with the person as their values blend in their chosen society. For health or for relief, the choice is theirs as is the choice for those around to share second hand, the smoke from another.

As smoke is a drug if ingested in a certain way, plants, herbs and chemicals may alter one's being in a similar way. For millenniums of time, chosen leaders have kept the secrets of medicines and their drugs to sooth the pain of another.

The medicine man, witch doctor or physician all play a role in healing and caring for another. Driving demons from a soul or infection from a body, caring and curing dance with the drugs of one's time.

The miracle in saving the life of another, radiates Love and service to all of the people in the chosen land. The spirit choosing the path of a healer dances with life, death, illness and pestilence for every person in his or her chosen land.

From research of compounds, plant life, organic and inorganic substances, drugs are created to serve in the

Love Dances

treatment of an ailment, or to prevent an ailment. Dancing with drugs changes as science advances new discoveries and ways to serve the care givers in healing, saving, extending and procreating lives for the chosen people.

The alteration of mind and body, created by a drug, may also go beyond the healing professions. Illicit or unneeded use for the high or alteration of a mind, soaring upward or crashing downward, goes unguided as drugs are used and abused by one seeking a retreat from one's own self.

The walls of pleasure lead to pain as one dances with drugs outside the guidance of healers. Some may be prescribed from too many healers or drug stores, while others, seeking their escape from themselves, choose the inner city connection or a stroll in a park to purchase whatever they think they are buying.

The hedonism and hope for acceptance of oneself is lonely and perpetuating as the habit of use continues until no self worth, no family or fortune remain. The symptoms of pain of non-acceptance, rejection and distorted personalization reign the destruction of the misuse of drugs as the path to death.

Dancing With Drugs & Smoke

Just as in mother nature, the drug jungle is like a wounded shark being attacked until death happens by the other sharks swimming in its sea. The turkeys may peck another baby turkey to death, without accepting the gift of life they could create in the universe, when all stands still and a spirit of a new turkey could choose its own life in the next year's egg.

The plants or large animals take all of the water from the watering hole during a drought, just as the continuing illicit use of drugs for people take life's blood. Other plants or gazelles may dance with death when there is no more water to sustain life and its freedoms, just as the brain cells or cells of a person's body are snuffed out with drugs.

God guides all of the chosen people with Love, honesty and spiritual acceptance for the choices along the path of their chosen life. As the angels in heaven guide and protect the new traveler to his or her kingdom, the same inner beauty and care radiate from within the spirit learning the lesson of Love, acceptance, pride and comfort with oneself.

Unconditional Love and honesty free insecurities, walls of protection and over-sensitivities of non-

LOVE DANCES

acceptance, removing all wants and desires for escapes, no matter what they may look like. Inner peace and harmony are created through this Love for oneself and then it is shared with all in the chosen land, as it is in heaven for eternity.

Dancing With Death

The dance of life begins at that split second in the universe when all stands still as a couple shares total Love for each other. At this exact moment a spirit has the opportunity to choose this life with these parents in this chosen land.

The path of life on earth begins at birth, when the inner spirit is born as a blessed child, in the true essence of God. The chosen life is filled with beauty, freedom and challenges.

This special life, and all of the experiences to come along its path, are so chosen by one's spirit. It made the ultimate connection during that split second when all in the universe and all in the heavens stood still.

Dancing with children is followed by the dances with adolescence, adulthood, parenthood and grandparenthood. The times of elation follow the times of sadness.

Love Dances

Love is shared. Love is lost. The perception of what is, grows as one chooses to build one's own unique walls hiding the open, honest, free spirit of the child within.

The heredity of the chosen ancestors blend with all in the chosen environment, as the spirit grows in concert with the God within. It casts its mark and learns its lessons during this chosen life.

The people, the marriage or marriages to another, children chosen as blessed by God and spirits choosing this family serve this special person during this time of living this life. The inner spirit connects among others for its chosen family, friends and all in its land.

Others choose solo living, reflecting a relationship with another of its own kind in service to God, their church, community, state, family or special friends. The beliefs, relationships and opportunities soar freely with Love, service to others and one's families as dances of choice.

The dances of successes, winning, being in one's magnificence and with pleasures and joy radiate in this chosen life. Dancing with one's sexuality and sharing the ultimate Love in sexual intimacy create new life.

Dances change as the spirit learns new steps. It

Dancing With Death

mimics and retains learned steps from the elder's and traditions of the land and with mother nature.

The dance of life is the dance of Loving, caring, uniting and creating the opportunity for the sharing of new spirits and their lives with all beings, in the chosen world. The dance of this chosen person is the same as the dance of the mocking birds rocking to certain beats.

The mocking birds dance among other voices in mating, with different nests to house their eggs. They create the opportunity for new mocking birds to join this special world of almond trees, honeysuckle blossoms and streams so still, yet so deep, that an entire world of new life is created and chosen during each split second in time.

As the birds, beasts and trees of the world search and share food, water and life with another of its kind, the spirits of all beings in the true essence of God, enjoy their chosen path, no matter how rocky or incredibly smooth it may seem. The choices of all in one's life represent a vision for a future, or the departure from the past and its walls that appeared to serve the soft, inner spirit connected to all other spirits in its chosen life line.

The dance of the walls close off the energy, freedom, passion for living and the Love to share with others in the

LOVE DANCES

chosen land. The higher and thicker the impressions grow, to protect oneself from the people, pain and the world outside, only wall off life itself from the inner spirit.

These walls keep one in the dance of insecurity, distrust, loneliness, victimization and pain. The choice, out of life, grows as each wall grows.

Each moment in the universe is a new moment and the opportunity to make a new choice. Just as in heaven, God shares the opportunity for the inner spirits to choose a new life with blessed parents of chosen people, golden eagles, crepe myrtle trees in their fluorescent glory or as calico cats.

Each spirit in every life enjoys the special gift of all it has chosen in its own special world. One dance follows another.

Some synchronized steps are the same steps as its parents danced, mating, parenting, working, playing and doing all it chooses to do when it dances in the chosen land. Other steps, this special person chooses to dance, are unique, maybe new with the changing times, maybe in rebellion from the traditions and cultures of the chosen people.

Dancing with life is dancing with death. After one is

born, he or she lives, Loves and experiences all of the dance steps of his or her chosen life.

Excitement, anticipation of new life and service to others reign supreme for people of all ages. Each memory shares and guides others across new thresholds in the beam of radiant white light with others, softly connected to other inner spirits.

The ultimate gift is to cherish each connection, so delicately, yet with complete trust, freedom and continuity of Love. This Love is embraced as the angels of the heavens embrace the spirits of a Loved one, no matter how young or old, leaving this chosen life and moving to another.

They serve and guide each other, adding new spirits among all spirits in the kingdom of heaven. The bond is made heart to heart, in the true spirit of God.

Life is here, then it is gone. The spirit chooses to continue its chosen path to its heaven, so blessed, so free, in the radiant beams of white, translucent light. This spirit is so soft, peaceful, so determined, with complete Love, in one's life, that only its vision changes.

The spirit never dies. It only changes its dance with death to a new dance of life. The cycle continues in Love

LOVE DANCES

and radiance with peace and harmony within each being, as a new life is chosen for this spirit.

One chooses another life with its own special dance, no matter what this dance looks like in which chosen land. The vision of inner peace, Love and harmony grows with each spirit as the feelings of Love, freedom, spiritual connections among each person are shared throughout every land and blessed by God for eternity.

Dancing With Peace & Harmony

Life comes and life goes in the chosen land, when one spirit chooses life and another chooses its heaven. In the true essence of God, a new blessed child arrives with a spirit within that is filled with Love, peace, harmony and a passion for its chosen life.

The dance of life creates wonderful experiences seeking the ultimate in Love and freedom to the spirit of this blessed child. From the first breath the child takes to the first step into its heaven, the spirit has chosen parents, friends, Lovers, elders and leaders of its own world.

As the reflections of life rock the baby to sleep under the twinkling of the stars, planets and celestial kingdoms, the spirit in the being enjoys all in its chosen world. The dawning of each new day, casts rays of sunlight and energy connecting with all others in the chosen land.

Special dances of learning, seeing, doing and being like another, embrace the inner spirit with the cultures,

LOVE DANCES

habits and action steps on its dance floor. The dance card is never full, but sometimes appears to have more gyrations happening with youths, young adults and new parents than is thought to be possible.

The same beautiful dance, yet with different steps, flows freely with Love, tenderness, compassion and caring in the grandparents and elders. The seniors of a chosen community dance in the twilight of their chosen lives with the soft, gentle power of success, unconditional Love, support and vision for their chosen family and special friends.

This dance culminates at the threshold of assistance to a Loved one entering a new chosen life. The dance soars in the crossing of another soft, inner spirit completing its chosen life. The departing vision dances in a gracious, regal way as it has chosen to join all in its heaven.

Sometimes the final steps of the beautiful dance of life ends as suddenly as it begins. Other spirits choose a long, last dance, at any age in human years, embracing lessons, transitions, strength and experiences for all in its chosen life.

The honesty of sharing each dance with a family member, close friends, acquaintances or another from a

Dancing With Peace & Harmony

different land, dances within the soul of one being connected for the first or many times with another. The kaleidoscope of threads of life, so softly, yet ever-so gently, connect one heart to another and another to the same heart. One unites with all in the universe.

The connection is strengthened with Love for oneself and in giving it to others, without greed, taking or for any other reason. True unconditional Love for oneself without the walls of expectation, excuses or defenses, is powerful, real and always within the soft inner spirit guiding the life's path.

The Love of oneself, acceptance in the radiance of one's heredity, environment and that which has been chosen, grows in the essence of God. One shares this Love with another, reflecting the true inner peace and harmony of the soul.

The spirits of all soar free as the birds in mother nature soar. Sometimes this flight is clumsy as the pelicans flap, bump and flop to the dance of flying with too many fishes under its bill.

The chorus of each critter in the land share the dances of peace and harmony. Sometimes the dance steps change as the vision of Love dances in the growl and the

Love Dances

snort of a young bull strutting his stuff for a new heifer, ignoring his dance of seduction. Then they join in that intimate dance, for that split second in the universe when all stands still and a new calf chooses a new life as a Jersey or Holstein calf, nine months or so later.

The withered corn is splattered by the first thunder shower of June in the north or December in the southern hemisphere. Each is caressed with water, like diamonds falling, as each drop of life for the peace and harmony of each stock and curly leaf.

The pollens, silks and ears of new life pulsate dance steps of fertilization when all stands still in the corn rows of the fields. The dance continues as the beautiful connection of future life occurs.

New life explodes in the rainbows chasing the thunder storm away. God joins the beautiful dance with mother nature in the corn fields of Australia, the Ukraine, Argentina and Iowa.

The dance of life continues in the creation. Kernels of corn grow as seeds for future corn stocks, as well as the excess to be shared with all of the earth's fruit and food for people and animals alike in the chosen land.

Dancing with peace and harmony begins within and

Dancing With Peace & Harmony

comforts securely one in his or her own chosen family, friends, animals, plants and land. The dance is unique and the steps are ever-changing as dancing with peace and harmony reigns supreme in the world and kingdoms of time eternity.

Dancing With Vision

God created the spirits of life, the worlds, universe and heaven. The special blessings to each person, place or thing are ever present and look as they are to look for all in each chosen land.

Families are chosen with beautiful legacies, tragedies, gifts and fortunes. One's life begins when a spirit, in the true essence of God, dances in a new life, when beings couple so romantically, so traditionally, so spontaneously, so dramatically.

The universe embraces a split second when all stands still in a true and total connection. The vision of life and the future occurs, whether planned or randomly, and a new spirit chooses its own dance of life.

The wonderful path of this chosen life is special and unknowing. Yet, this special gift of the spirit within is a gift of total choice, for each moment throughout time.

What has been, is the dance of perception as the

dance of all that had appeared to be. One person tells the story differently from another, whether he or she is across the kitchen table, across the Red Sea or Pacific Ocean.

Each tale shared with another, can be told with a style of intrigue, victimization, joy, pain or on and on. The medias of life cast their spells with perceptions of each story told.

The drama of lives from one to another grow and encompass entire states of people in other lands. They dance with reverberations in peculiar, sometimes predictable ways of life, death, happiness and winning.

One's boredom creates folderol. Just as the boy cries wolf time and time again, putting all to sleep in the village of his chosen land.

Guarding his flock reflected his own life. He chose to excite, when no excitement was there.

He chose the wall of attention, dramatizing this possible event. As the arrival of the wolf was created, so was his deception, distortion, dishonesty and doom.

The spirit of the wolf chose her or his own dance with the sheep of this wolf's world. Caring for her or his cubs in providing lamb chops for the chosen wolf pack, is a wonderful dance of life, for one, and the freedom of a

Love Dances

new life for another.

Different stories are wonderful, boring for one, tragic for some, successful for another, freeing for others. Just as people, dancing with people from other lands, the dancing with vision soars beyond one's own perceptions, judgments, walls and personalizations.

Freeing the inner spirits of all beings in every land creates Love, peace and harmony for everyone and everything. Dancing with vision is dancing in the translucent, white light of spiritual Love.

The spirit within every soul guides our chosen paths of life. The blessed child chooses all at that split second in the universe when it connects with parents, elders, church leaders, television commentators and others in the chosen land.

The dance of life chooses the dance of learning, sharing, creating memories, and a wonderful future for oneself and all throughout the world. Sharing the dance of Love grows as the inner spirit grows in the true essence of God.

Spirituality is here, everywhere. The Love within and about is the spiritual connection, softly, gently sharing our oneness with another.

Dancing With Vision

Taking care of the environment in every chosen land, serving others as they have never been served, Loving unconditionally oneself and all others, and freeing every person, place or thing, creates a spiritual vision guiding all, as God guides all.

Each spirit shares this beautiful dance for eternity, dancing with vision.

ORDER TODAY!

Love Dances

Please send me ____ copy(ies) of **LOVE DANCES** by **Van V. Heffner** at $12.95 per copy plus US $3.00 shipping and handling per order. I enclose ___check, ___money order, or please charge my bank card: ___VISA ___MC ___AMEX. Nevada residents please add appropriate sales tax.

Name _____

Address _____

City _____ State _____ Zip _____

Card # _____ Exp. _____

Signature _____

Mail orders to:　　　　H&A Publishing Company
　　　　　　　　　　　4820 Alpine Place
　　　　　　　　　　　Suite B202
　　　　　　　　　　　Las Vegas, NV 89107

or Fax to:　　　　　　702-878-5009
(Credit card only)